D0956089

TEACH BEYOND YOUR REACH

An Instructor's Guide to Developing and Running Successful DISTANCE LEARNING Classes, Workshops, Training Sessions and More

Robin Neidorf

Information Today, Inc.
Medford, New Jersey

First Printing, 2006

Teach Beyond Your Reach: An Instructor's Guide to Developing and Running Successful Distance Learning Classes, Workshops, Training Sessions and More

Library of Congress Cataloging-in-Publication Data

Neidorf, Robin.
Teach beyond your reach : an instructor's guide to developing and running successful distance learning classes, workshops, training sessions and more / Robin Neidorf.
p. cm.
Includes bibliographical references and index.
ISBN 0-910965-73-0
1. Distance education. 2. Teacher-student relationships. I. Title.
LC5800.N45 2006
371.35--dc22

2006006263

Printed and bound in the United States of America

President and CEO: Thomas H. Hogan, Sr.
Editor-in-Chief and Publisher: John B. Bryans
Managing Editor: Amy M. Reeve
VP Graphics and Production: M. Heide Dengler
Book Designer: Kara Mia Jalkowski
Cover Designer: Michele Quinn
Copyeditor: Bonnie Freeman
Proofreader: Barbara Brynko
Indexer: Sharon Hughes

Contents

Figures, Tables, and Worksheets

Acknowledgments

The usual cast of thousands has contributed to the ideas in this book. I'm grateful to many individuals and organizations for their trust in me and their willingness to co-create learning experiences with me.

The following people generously gave of their time and shared expertise by granting interviews, sharing resources, pointing me in the right direction, and providing assistance and support of many kinds: Michael Allen, Jim Austin, Monique Cuvelier, Kim Dority, Linda MacCauley Freeman, Christine Hamilton-Pennell, Jean Hanson, Rabbi Hayim Herring, Andrea Jarrell, Jennifer Kaplan, Jan Knight, William Males, Heather Martin, Serena Pelowski, Heidi Pliam, Mark Rossman, Karen Steinhilber, Wendy Weiner, the workshop presenters of Sloan-C, my terrific colleagues on the discussion list for the Association for Independent Information Professionals (AIIP), and my writing e-buddies in the Bennington Collective.

The following organizations and people have helped me become a better instructor, writer, thinker, and mensch by giving me opportunities to test ideas and to stumble as well as succeed: the Bennington Writing Seminars; Compleat Scholar at the University of Minnesota; JSkyway; Synagogues: Transformation and Renewal (STAR); University of Phoenix; University of Gävle; and my writing instructors and mentors, particularly Sven Birkerts, Susan Cheever, and Morgan Grayce Willow.

I could not have completed this book—or really much of anything in my life—without the support of my husband, Andrew Sullivan, and our daughter, Talia Sullivan Neidorf.

To the countless students who have allowed me to work with them and change their thinking and sometimes their lives—my gratitude.

To my colleagues in the field of instruction—my best wishes.

Introduction

Those Who Can, Teach

Becoming a Teacher

My first teaching opportunity came when I was still in high school. I was a math tutor, working with junior high students struggling with algebra. In a one-on-one setting, often lounging with my students on their bedroom floors, I explained polynomial functions and abstract numbers. I also answered questions about life beyond eighth grade graduation. From the lofty distance of three years, I could reflect on how I had risen to the challenge of high school. My willingness to talk and to respond to their questions helped several of them express and then ease their fears about moving into the next stage of their education.

From that first experience in that most intimate setting, I've expanded my teaching to classrooms, virtual and traditional. I've taught a few hundred students of varying skills and interests, covering topics including college composition, Web-based business research techniques, nonprofit marketing and branding, creative writing, and more. My writing and composition students in particular seem to thrive under my watch. Together we untangle the mysteries of English grammar while shaping ideas through the power of written words.

I never see most of my students and only rarely speak to any of them on the telephone. We communicate primarily through asynchronous discussion, e-mail, and the occasional instant messenger session; they send assignments via Web depository or e-mail, and I respond digitally with detailed feedback. Yet I find that in many ways the relationships we have are not altogether different from those I had as a math tutor. I am doing much more than serving as a conduit to the mastery of a specific subject or skill. Rather, I am changing the way they think about themselves and interact with their entire world. I am helping them build confidence, agree to take risks, and believe in themselves and their ability to perform in a quickly changing world.

When I am teaching, whether face to face or on opposite sides of the world, I am engaged in one of the most rewarding, challenging, and connected roles I take on in my busy life.

Why Write This Book?

I came to distance learning initially with some skepticism. Despite earning my own master's degree in creative writing through a low-residency program (a hybrid form of distance education involving brief on-campus periods followed by six-month stretches of work through the mail with a mentor), I wasn't convinced that distance methods could adequately serve the needs of a dynamic classroom. From my comic-book-reading days, I remembered the "Draw me!" ads offering to train me to be an artist although I could barely draw a 3-D cube with any degree of accuracy. Was it really possible to deliver high-quality learning experiences if I couldn't see and immediately respond to my students?

When I first explored the possibilities of distance learning early in 2002, my experience included teaching in a live classroom as well as years of experience (naturally) on the other side of the gradebook. I was comfortable with traditional classrooms, and so I took them as the norm against which distance learning would have to be measured. When teaching in front of a class, I knew (more or less) what to expect and how to prepare. I knew how to read expressions, think on my feet, adapt, take a little more time with a challenging topic, or allow an unexpectedly profound discussion to run long. How could an online classroom ever compare?

Since then, I've taught dozens of courses through a variety of distance-learning formats. I've learned how to adapt both what I teach and how I teach so that I maximize the features and benefits of different learning environments. I've learned more about learning styles, as well as my own strengths and weaknesses as an instructor. Most important, I've become more conscious of what I need to do to deliver an engaging, educational course—a development that has had a deep, positive impact on all my teaching, no matter what the venue.

My Experiences with Distance Learning

In 1996, I graduated with a master's degree in creative writing with the inaugural class of the Bennington Writing Seminars (BWS) at Bennington College in Vermont. As mentioned earlier, BWS is based on a low-residency format: four semesters of one-on-one work through the mail with writing mentors, interspersed with "residencies" in January and June, when we participated in workshops, lectures, and graduation for the outgoing class. At the time, there were only half a dozen low-residency master's programs in writing in the country; today there are more than 30, with new ones being established each year.

Following graduation, I began teaching occasionally in traditional classrooms, primarily through the adult enrichment program at the University of Minnesota in Minneapolis. A couple of years later, I started my research and communications business, which enabled me to start developing and conducting customized training programs for clients in business research, public relations basics, audience-focused communication, and more. When I couldn't travel to a client site, we would naturally move to a teleconference format. I began to become more interested in finding other ways to reach geographically remote audiences.

In 1999, I joined an online writer's group for BWS alumni. Although I've never met the majority of the writers in the group, our exchanges of both writing and the woes of the artistic struggle have allowed us to develop very close relationships. One of my dear colleagues in this group is William Males, a lecturer at the University of Gävle in Sweden, where he lives. Before we ever met face to face, William invited me to become a co-teacher in his Creative Writing in English course, taught online under the auspices of his university.

Late in 2001 and early in 2002, my business (and many others) was in a slow mode. Seeking additional income sources, I responded to an online faculty recruitment advertisement from the University of Phoenix Online. I was accepted into the intensive one-month training program, and I successfully taught my first class—Essentials of College Writing—at the University of Phoenix in August 2002.

By the middle of 2003, I was eagerly looking for more ways to incorporate distance-learning principles into my consulting practice. I found the perfect opportunity in my relationship with a national nonprofit, Synagogues: Transformation and Renewal (STAR). STAR provides training, education, and capacity building for synagogues and their leaders through its programs. As STAR's communications consultant, I've been charged with the exciting and challenging task of creating and reviewing distance-learning opportunities for rabbis, synagogue professionals, and volunteers in a variety of key areas—including synagogue marketing, which I not only develop but teach as well.

There are other elements of my professional and personal life that make distance learning a perfect arena in which to play, but these primary touch points in my history will help you understand the basis for my approach to distance instruction.

Teaching through distance learning is just as rewarding as teaching in a traditional classroom setting (or even more so). I teach through distance learning in part because flexible formats enable me to work with students I wouldn't otherwise be able to reach and to add classes to an already busy schedule. The students I encounter through distance learning have widely diverse backgrounds, abilities, and needs, bringing a new richness to my own experiences as an instructor.

Still, these benefits weren't achieved simply through migrating to a distance-learning platform. Making distance learning such a positive experience for my students and me has taken focus, attention, training, and a willingness to experiment. Taking advantage of distance learning has made me take a critical look at every element of my formal and informal teaching and to think differently about exactly what I'm offering students.

When I was first invited to teach a seminar in a traditional classroom setting, I had only one decision to make: What was I going to present, based on the requested topic and the knowledge level of the students? Now that I'm developing distance-learning offerings, I have an entire host of additional decisions to make, including which platform to use, how to format materials, which ways to integrate technology to enhance the learning experience, and how to manage and guide a student's "classroom" experience.

The biggest surprise for me in the shift from classroom to distance has been the relationships I have with my distance students. From the moment I conceive an idea for a possible distance-learning program, the students are present. As I craft objectives, activities, lesson plans, the arc of a learning experience, the integration of technology, and even the content of assignments, I am in silent dialogue with the students who live in my head—asking questions, pointing out inconsistencies in the classroom experience, giving me the deer-in-the-headlights stare because I've failed to provide the background information they need to complete an assignment.

In distance learning, ironically, the students are *always* present.

I love that connection with students and the potential for creating meaningful change (in them) and exchange (between us). So many talented instructors and potential instructors dismiss the idea of distance learning because the traditional classroom is their norm, as it was for me before I started teaching at a distance. They assume, as I did, that it's too difficult or even impossible to craft those connections without being in a face-to-face environment. My hope is that this book will help you expand your ideas about creative possibilities in distance learning and give you the practical knowledge you need to make it happen at the same time.

But What Exactly *Is* Distance Learning?

Does distance learning mean Web-based education? Correspondence courses? Self-paced activities? Virtual teams? Teleconferences? Satellite courses? Interactive video? Short, easy answer: Any and all of the above. Distance learning is more visible today than ever before because of the way the Internet has become embedded in corporate, academic, and consumer life. But it has existed longer than the Web, and if, as some doom-and-gloomers predict, the Web one day collapses under the monstrous weight of its unsupportable growth, distance learning will continue to be a viable option for education of all kinds.

But it's true that Web-based education dominates the current development in the field because of its many advantages for instructors, developers, and students. Even within the category of Web-based classrooms, we can find plenty of variation in learning platforms and instructional approaches. A "Webinar" usually refers to a real-time Web-based presentation, with or without viewer interaction. Web-based classrooms can be synchronous (e.g., real-time chat rooms) or asynchronous (e.g., threaded discussions in a dedicated space or forum). Instructional models have even been built around downloadable e-books, with interaction provided through e-mail.

In other words, you have options. By uncoupling instruction from the traditional classroom restrictions of time and place, you have an opportunity to focus on the following questions:

- What information and knowledge do you want to share with students?
- What outcomes do you want your students to achieve (what should they be able to say, think, or do as a result of the learning experience)?
- What is the best combination of instructor resources, student resources, materials, technology, and expense to achieve a successful outcome?

This book will help you answer these questions and develop the materials, resources, tools, and processes you need to act on your answers. And unlike other resources on distance education, this book does not assume you will choose a Web-based platform, or even a technology-driven platform, on which to teach. You may find that printed materials and snail mail work just as well to accomplish your goals and create a satisfying experience for you and your students.

Who Should Read This Book?

This book is written by an instructor for instructors. It is intended primarily for those who are interested in enhancing their teaching skills, broadening their student pool, or challenging their own assumptions about what goes into a functional classroom, and for those who are just plain intrigued by the possibilities of distance learning but want a guided approach to make it work for them.

The pressure on institutions and instructors to find ways to develop and deliver effective distance learning is intensifying. Hardly a university exists that isn't asking instructors to incorporate an online component into their courses, as well as create online-only offerings to maximize the reach of the institution. Consultants, trainers, and topic experts are exploring distance learning as a way to expand their reach (and potential revenue sources) while minimizing airport time. Associations, facing increasing competition for their members' time, dues, and loyalty, are turning to distance learning as a way to add value to their memberships; they can offer training, professional development, and networking opportunities that members can access at their convenience, without the expense and hassle of attending an on-site meeting or conference. And all of these institutions need instructors who are creative, confident in their choice of distance-learning tools, and ready to meet the needs of a wide range of students.

Different Types of Readers: How to Use This Book

This information will help you understand how to incorporate this book into your planning and development, based on your particular situation and needs.

If you are

- Teaching at a college or university

Then you probably

- Are required to use a specific platform (e.g., WebCT, Blackboard, proprietary, or other)
- Have access to instructional design support
- Have access to technical support
- Have experience teaching in traditional classrooms

And you can use this book to

- Learn to adapt your teaching style to a distance format
- Learn what questions to ask and how to present your ideas and "wish list" to design and technical specialists
- Get fresh ideas on teaching and how to best help students of all kinds

If you are

- Part of a small or midsize business

Then you probably

- Have a limited budget
- Do not have access to a high-cost, feature-rich platform
- Are also responsible at some level for marketing your courses

And you can use this book to

- Understand how to apply the concepts of distance learning in course design
- Identify, select, and implement low-cost and low-tech options effectively
- Gain perspective on audiences and learners and understand how to deliver (and market) something they want and need

If you are

- An independent consultant, freelance instructor, or other solo practitioner

Then you probably

- Have a minuscule budget
- Have deep topic expertise but limited (if any) access to other kinds of expertise
- Need to market your course to survive

And you can use this book to

- Learn how to package your knowledge in course content
- Learn how to instruct students rather than simply talk about what you know
- Get a sense of what your market might look like and need in an instructional setting

- Understand the partnerships you may need to teach a course effectively
- Identify low-cost options for launching and testing a course "product"
- Make decisions about which tools and methods to use to deliver distance education

If you are

- Supporting instructors in their distance education endeavors (e.g., you are a training company or department, college dean, technical expert, instructional designer, student support services provider, or platform provider)

Then you probably

- Work with others who will be instructing students
- Need to convince instructors at times to move out of their comfort zone and think differently about instruction
- Mentor or coach instructors to be successful in new areas and with new skill sets

And you can use this book to

- Create shared knowledge with your instructors about scope of work, creative possibilities, content development, audience, and more
- Provide instructors with step-by-step guidance in moving to a distance-learning environment
- Help instructors develop better skills in working with students, organizing their courses, and being effective teachers

If you are

- A decision maker for an association, business, organization, or other entity

Then you probably

- Need to find effective ways to enhance the value of your entity to your audiences (members, employees, beneficiaries, etc.)

And you can use this book to

- Understand the ways distance education offerings may enhance your overall structure by offering high-quality, high-touch, user-focused experiences on more flexible and cost-effective terms than traditional classrooms, conferences, publications, or other methods can

How This Book Is Organized

This book is not designed to be a "soup to nuts" compendium of steps in implementing a distance-learning program. You will not learn how to develop Web pages, install or troubleshoot software, provide student support services, or fulfill other critical needs in developing and delivering an effective distance-learning program. There are many other books and resources you can turn to for that kind of assistance (although in my opinion, you have enough to do to teach without needing to learn to create a Web page, too). The supplementary reading list in Appendix A provides sources of additional practical guidance beyond the scope of planning and instruction, and other resources can be found at the companion Web site for this book: www.electric-muse.com/tbyr.asp. But go only as deeply as you feel compelled to go in these other areas. Learn enough to be a good partner to those who have the passion for software or support services that you have for instruction.

One of the underlying themes of this book is that distance learning is best created in collaboration with others. I do not believe it is even possible to excel at performing all of the roles that go into a successful distance-learning program. So you need to know going into it that this book focuses strictly on the requirements for instruction and points out where you need to partner with others to create the best possible educational environment for you and your students.

Content Overview: It's All About Interaction

The core of learning is interaction.

In traditional classrooms, interaction takes place primarily in a face-to-face setting—a classroom usually, or perhaps team meetings or instructor conferences. It's what most of us are used to and, at some unconscious level, expect.

In distance learning, interaction is still the beating heart of the educational experience. The interaction, however, occurs at a temporal and spatial disconnect. Learners, instructor, content, and social community are no longer contained within the same four walls at the same time. Yet learning occurs. The job of the instructor is to create the right conditions for interaction with the instructor, content, and learning peers, regardless of the distance between the elements.

Ultimately, the instructor does not create learning (whew!); the instructor can create only the environment, distant or not, in which learning can be *co-created* through the *interaction with content, peers,* and *instructor* (see Figure I.1).

The tools of distance learning are the media through which these interactions are enabled. Chapter 1 discusses the tools available for distance learning and suggests how they may be used, individually and in concert with one another.

Best practices in instruction focus on the learner rather than on the content. Chapter 2 describes what the distance population looks like and how it behaves. By focusing on adult students, this chapter lays out different learning styles, generational differences, and attitudes toward education that can make a difference in how students enter your class, work with you and the material, and communicate their educational goals.

Chapters 3 and 4 focus on creating content for distance learning that encourages interaction while achieving learning objectives. Chapter 3 guides you through the questions and processes that will help you create

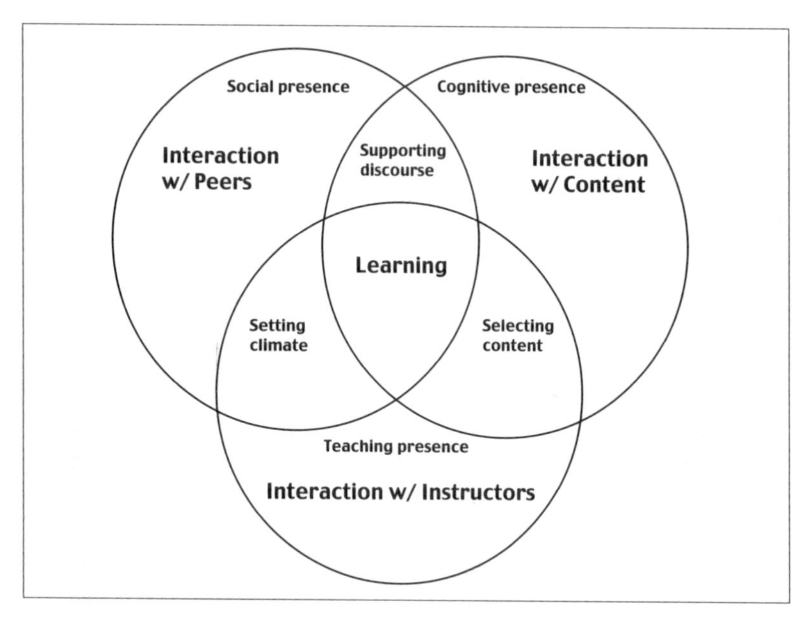

Figure I.1 Interaction with content, instructor, and peers. The three kinds of interaction are what co-create an effective learning experience. (*Used with permission from Swan, Karen. (2003). "Learning Effectiveness: What the Research Tells Us," in* Elements of Quality Online Education: Practice and Direction. *Sloan-C: Needham, MA. Additional information is available at www.sloan-c.org.*)

the overall course design, while Chapter 4 offers detailed information on the actual craft and implementation of course content elements such as lectures, presentations, assignments, and so on.

The role of the instructor in a distance-learning environment can be neither "sage on the stage" nor "guide on the side." Depending on the degree of comfort your students have with distance learning, your own pedagogical style, the tools you have at hand, and the objectives of the course, you may find yourself taking on any combination of many different roles: mentor, coach, instructor, facilitator, referee, trainer, and even shoulder to cry on.

In a traditional classroom, expectations of the instructor are fairly clear, particularly if all participants have been raised in similar cultures. Everyone agrees what the words "instructor," "student," "classroom," "performance," and "you are on the verge of failing" mean. Move into a distance-learning environment, though, and expectations become much more amorphous. Often, instructors who are new to distance learning are surprised to find that their interactions with learners are quite a bit more intense and intimate than they might be in a traditional classroom and that they lead to close and rewarding relationships of mutual development. As exhilarating as such an experience can be for an instructor, this degree of intimacy with students can require skill development in areas not previously considered to be part of your pedagogy—for instance, in motivational skills or boundary setting.

On the other hand, instructors are sometimes surprised at how much effort they have to make just to hear a peep out of some of their students. The primacy of interaction in a successful distance-learning environment requires that instructors prepare students to interact. This is harder than it sounds. Years of conditioning through everything from lecture-hall classes to television viewing have not prepared students for active engagement with instructors, materials, or each other. Motivation and creative use of interactive tools will be essential to helping students succeed. Satisfied distance-learning students are those who have had appropriate expectations raised, are trained to get the most out of the experience, and are encouraged, coached, prodded, and urged to be as active as possible in their own education.

Chapter 5 provides insight and ideas for managing the distance-learning "classroom" and helping your students interact effectively with you to maximize their learning. You will also find tips and wisdom from the field about what to expect and how to foster the kinds of interaction that make great learning possible. Chapter 6 provides guidance on getting to know your students as individual learners, working with their strengths and weaknesses, and motivating them to their peak performance through mentoring and feedback.

We humans are social creatures. The importance of collaborative work in creating an effective distance-learning environment has been documented in study after study. Foster positive group interaction and your students will reap the benefits, even if they grumble about the additional challenges that participating in a community may create.

Fostering positive group interaction is also harder than it may first seem. The mandate to create community seems nonsensical in the face of the physical distances separating the learners and their limited means of getting to know one another on a personal level. Distance programs tend to attract a diverse group of students, which makes it even more challenging—yet vital—to establish common ground for group bonding. More subtly, the dominant culture of education is one of competition rather than collaboration; distance-learning instructors have to shift student expectations from eyeing one another suspiciously to treating each other as a valued part of the process.

Of all the kinds of interactions that distance instruction threw at me, building a community of learners was one of the hardest to handle. At first I didn't see the value of collaborative work, in part because in my experience as a learner, interaction with peers has never been my preference. Throughout my schooling, I dreaded participating in group projects and invariably wanted to go into my corner and work on my own. I've found, however, that the work I put into helping the students develop teams and mutually supportive relationships brings rich rewards to everyone. Distance-learning classes are usually diverse in terms of learner experience, background, skills, and perspective. The work we do together, as a collaborative community, adds to the education of everyone ... including the instructor.

Of course, chemistry is always a bit uncertain, but an instructor can find ways to improve the odds of creating a bit of interpersonal magic. Chapter 7 introduces the keys for creating effective learning communities at a distance.

Distance learning is fundamentally a collaborative enterprise. You can be an outstanding instructor, but without assistance and support from knowledgeable partners, it's difficult to offer high-quality distance education. This book is also a useful tool to help decision makers (including administrators, deans, executive directors, and others) and supporting experts (Web designers, technical support folks, instructional designers, and even marketing staff) understand what you are trying to create and how they can best contribute to the process.

To create a successful team, first it is important to create a shared understanding of the place, purpose, and objectives of a distance-learning program. Chapter 8 is designed to serve as a stand-alone "state of the environment" review of the challenges, potential, and collaborative roles involved in distance learning. For individual instructors, this chapter ties the details of the book into the broader context of the practical world of business education, personal enrichment, and academia. You will also find this chapter helpful as preliminary reading for the entire team involved in distance learning—including students. Use the worksheet and discussion guide at the end of Chapter 8 to establish a shared understanding of your particular situation within the cultural, social, academic, professional, and technical context of distance learning.

Those Who Can, Teach ... Beyond Their Reach

Not every expert can teach. We've all had classes and lectures in which the sage on the stage clearly knew her "stuff" but just as clearly didn't have a clue about how to communicate—let alone teach—competence in said stuff. Teaching is a skill that is too often overlooked or underestimated.

Connection, communication, motivation, response: All these are required for effective instruction, above and beyond knowledge of the specific subject to be taught. In fact, I've found that I can cram to gain subject knowledge when necessary, but I cannot fake the core skills that allow me to create connections with students, communicate with them, and motivate them to succeed.

Because distance instruction takes us out of a comfortable environment and throws us into an unfamiliar one, it gives us the opportunity to challenge every expectation we may have about why, to whom, and how to teach. The concepts and processes covered in this book will help you create and deliver effective distance-learning programs. They likely will also help you become a more effective instructor in traditional environments. If most of your own education has been in competitive environments that focus on finding errors, teaching to the test, and mastering skills rather than building knowledge, you will discover a new model in these pages. Learner-centric teaching, on which successful distance-learning programs are based, puts the learner's needs, skills, and strengths at the heart of the classroom experience. It recognizes the learner's need to receive positive reinforcement even while accepting correction. At its best, it creates a safe place for people to try out new ideas and new skills, make unique human connections, and discover their own potential.

So explore the possibilities of distance education to teach management strategy, technical topics, poetry, higher math, computer programming, graphic design, parenting skills, foreign language, Web development, literature, music history—even how to create and deliver effective distance-learning courses.

Whatever your expertise, and whatever your passion for instruction and connecting with students, open your arms and your creative sense of what's possible. Find the distance venues and methods that work for you, and teach beyond your reach.

Chapter 1

New Tools of the Trade

"Each medium, independent of the content it mediates, has its own intrinsic effects which are its unique message."

– Marshall McLuhan, *Understanding Media: The Extensions of Man*

In 1964, Marshall McLuhan first articulated what has become a mantra of the Information Age: The medium is the message. The tools that support the interactions of your distance-learning program are more than a collection of functions and features. Your choice of tools and how you use them will impact which students come to you, how successful they are, and the subtle messages you project about the value, purpose, and goals of your program.

The role of media in how information is received, absorbed, and processed should not be underestimated. Consider a somewhat extreme example:

> **Scenario 1:** Employee enters the human resources (HR) director's office for a private meeting. The HR director says, "Jane, you've been doing an outstanding job. As you know, though, we're moving toward a complete restructuring of your department, and your particular job is going to be eliminated. I'd like to talk with you about the options, for both accepting severance and utilizing our job search services."
>
> **Scenario 2:** Employee receives an e-mail from the HR director, which states:

Subject line: We need to meet

Jane, you've been doing an outstanding job. As you know, though, we're moving toward a complete restructuring of your department, and your particular job is going to be eliminated. I'd like to talk with you about the options, for both accepting severance and utilizing our job search services.

Sam Smith
Director of Human Resources

It's a bad day in either case, but put yourself in Jane's position: Which communication makes you more willing to work with the person presenting the information? Same exact words, but the impact is quite different if they're said in person rather than read in an e-mail. The medium is an inextricable component of what is communicated.

A distance-learning instructor needs to have a general understanding of the following factors:

- Tools potentially available
- Impact of the choice of tools on the delivery of a course and on both student and instructor satisfaction
- Project budget
- Applicability of available tools to the needs of a particular project

This chapter will discuss the characteristics, pros, and cons of the various tools a distance instructor may choose to use, from least complex to most complex.

Least-Complex Tools

Do you want to start your adventure into distance learning with minimal expense and dependence on technology? Consider these tools, which enable you to work with students around the globe yet do not require huge investments in development or infrastructure.

Snail-Mail Correspondence

The original distance-learning program was the correspondence-by-mail course. It's a model that still works and has its rightful place in your bag of tricks.

When I first discussed my ideas for this book with my editor, I mentioned the continuing use of snail mail as a distance-learning tool. "Is anyone still using *that*?" he asked. Sure! Real, tangible paper is invaluable for making handwritten notes on an assignment and exchanging materials that do not travel well by digital methods (like original artwork), and nothing, but nothing, in the digital world can match "real" mail for permanence. I completed my master's degree in creative writing through the Bennington Writing Seminar's low-residency program, organized around monthly packets of writing mailed back and forth between student and writing mentor. Although nearly 10 years have passed since I completed that degree, I still have every single letter my instructors sent to me. Had I received their comments via digital means, I know I would not have them anymore. The instruction that I was not ready for 10 years ago is now a valued part of my self-awareness as a developing writer.

Mail continues to have its place and special uses, despite the shift many of us have made to communicate electronically. In fact, the rise of electronic communication has enhanced the status of "real" mail as the medium to use when staying power matters.

E-mail Correspondence

Shift from the post office to postoffice.com, and the character and function of correspondence change in both large and small ways. E-mail is such an integral part of our everyday world that it's hard to remember when it was rather novel and unsettling. (I distinctly remember the first time I e-mailed an article to an editor rather than faxing it or dropping it off; we were both giddy with the thrill and completely amazed that it worked.)

A Quick View of Snail Mail

Pros: Universally accessible. An important form of personal touch in a context that can otherwise be impersonal. Very inexpensive in both implementation and usage.
Cons: Snail mail moves like, well, a snail. Not as effective for communication among multiple parties. Long delays between sending, receiving, and responding can be an instructional challenge.
Works best for: Mentored relationships that require primarily a one-on-one interaction between a student and an instructor.
Messages it sends: The work is worth devoting time to; don't rush, but rather consider how to create something worth printing, copying, and mailing.

E-mail is an instructional tool used in just about every educational environment you can think of today. When considering e-mail as a planned component of a distance-learning program, however, think in terms of how it can build relationships among members of a group as well as between an instructor and a student.

It is possible to base an entire distance-learning program solely on the use of e-mail, just as instructors have based distance-learning programs solely on traditional correspondence. The advantage of e-mail over snail mail, in addition to speed, is the relative ease of adding other people into a dialogue, creating opportunity for shared communal experiences rather than just one-on-one interactions.

Teleconference

I admit that I'm not the world's biggest fan of teleconferencing, although I've led and participated in more teleconferences that I care to count. With all the shifts that have taken place in the telecommunications industry, you can find teleconferencing packages ranging from free to pricey. Free systems (like FreeConference.com) generally require users to pay long-distance charges to connect to the teleconference (although, with so many low-cost plans available, the overall expense may

A Quick View of E-mail

Pros: Almost universally accessible. Fast response with the ability to create group discussion. An almost expected component of any professional relationship today. Free, or at least, very inexpensive.
Cons: E-mail may encourage "off the cuff" responses from both student and instructor. Managing group dialogue can be challenging, especially if responses run long. Many individuals feel overwhelmed by e-mail, especially with spam so rampant, and may tune out e-mail communications.
Works best for: Smaller discussion groups (five or so people) and as an integrated component of other distance media. Also appropriate for one-on-one instruction, turning in assignments, informal instruction or mentoring, etc.
Messages it sends: Quick, easy, and convenient.

still be negligible). On the high end are companies that can incorporate Web-based features into a teleconference (creating a Webinar), toll-free access codes, caller blocking, and a host of other features. Depending on the features selected and the frequency of use, these systems can range in price from 35 cents up to several dollars per person per minute.

For distance-learning programs, teleconferences are best kept relatively short (an hour or less) and focused on a single topic. Know that those on the call are very likely multitasking—checking e-mail, eating lunch, tidying their desks, working on crossword puzzles—which makes for less-than-optimal learning conditions. Some instructors have truly mastered this form and are adept at fielding questions from a large number of participants, all while hitting their learning objectives and creating a positive experience for everyone. I find that with more than half a dozen participants on the call, I can easily get confused as to who is talking at any one time. Time zones are also a challenge, even if all the participants are within the continental U.S.

On the upside, however, teleconferencing involves little or no learning curve (most adults know how to dial a telephone). A teleconference can also be an effective "kick-off" component to a distance-learning program that will otherwise take place online or in another format that lacks immediacy. It can be a comfortable, familiar introduction to what might otherwise feel like an impersonal experience. Teleconferences are good opportunities for minilectures, orientation, immediate questions about course work, and team meetings.

A Quick View of Teleconferencing

Pros: Immediacy of human interaction. Relatively inexpensive, and no learning curve. A Web component can accompany a teleconference, depending on the conference provider.
Cons: Inflexible format. Difficult to create dialogue among many participants. Requires everyone to be on the call at the same time (although it is possible to archive audio and Web component(s) to replay later).
Works best for: Short presentations and team projects.
Messages it sends: Easy and convenient; content may not be too in-depth (if teleconference is a stand-alone offering) and is largely presentational rather than interactive.

Synchronous Chat

Move the teleconference online and you have synchronous chat, which brings multiple users into a secure online space for immediate give-and-take. Like teleconferencing, chat—or instant messaging (IM)—requires all participants to be available at the same time. The results of an IM session are easy to archive for later review.

Many popular Internet service providers make chat space available, with free registration to establish a user name and an IM account; depending on the provider, this service may involve advertising components. Microsoft is just one of the companies offering free downloads and

Web-based IM (no software downloading required); most of the other major players in Internet software and access, such as AOL, Yahoo! and others, also provide IM. All participants in a given IM session must use the same system to conduct a chat session.

Synchronous chat is a native language of teens, but older folks (which in tech terms means anyone born before 1975) can find it difficult to follow multiple chatters. The limitations of the software mean that responses from chatters can be delayed, resulting in an online dialogue that is out of sync. Still, for immediate questions and task-oriented group meetings, chat can get the job done.

A Quick View of Synchronous Chat (Instant Messaging)

Pros: Free in its basic form. Offers immediacy, ability to archive results, and availability of Web-based resources during chat for reference and research. Some instant messaging (IM) systems can be accessed with a cellphone or a palmtop computer, making IM extremely portable.

Cons: The learning curve, and even downloading the software and setting up a free account, can be a challenge for a newbie. Requires everyone to be online at the same time, to have a functional account, and to have access to compatible IM systems and reliable Internet access. In-depth discussion among many participants can be hard to follow. Because of security restrictions, participants logging in from business or government locations may not be able to use free IM tools.

Works best for: Focused team projects, quick one-on-one updates, or just-in-time coaching.

Messages it sends: "Right now" access, at the expense of depth.

I often use IM in my business to discuss project details with partners in Europe and the Middle East as well as throughout North America; my students often use IM to conduct meetings about team assignments, to divide assignments, and to ask each other questions that arise about assignments or projects. I've also used chat to connect with support services, including those associated with distance learning and to troubleshoot and resolve issues that inevitably come up while using complex software and tools.

Midrange Tools

Tools that are considered midrange in complexity may require a bit more assistance from an expert to function effectively. Still, these are tools that most instructors can build learning experiences around with minimal expense and investment in the tool itself.

Asynchronous Discussion

When participants can access class discussion any time, from anywhere they have a computer connected to the Internet, that's asynchronous discussion (AD). AD is the heart and soul of many distance-learning programs. Proprietary Web-based course management systems (see "Most-Complex Tools," to follow) incorporate AD as part of their standard feature sets, and the University of Phoenix Online, where I teach communications courses, has built its entire (massive) online delivery system around AD and a secure newsgroup system.

But AD doesn't need to be complex or expensive. Many vendors and services offer AD capabilities through discussion forums, listservs, newsgroups, and the like. As the technology evolves, the distinctions among the various forms of AD become less important from the user's perspective.

The following types of AD are available:

- **Forum or bulletin board:** Requires participants to visit the discussion host to participate in the dialogue (see Figure 1.1).
- **Listserv:** Delivers all discussion to the participants' e-mail. Many systems also create a Web-based archive that functions much like a bulletin board so users can log in to view and respond to postings.

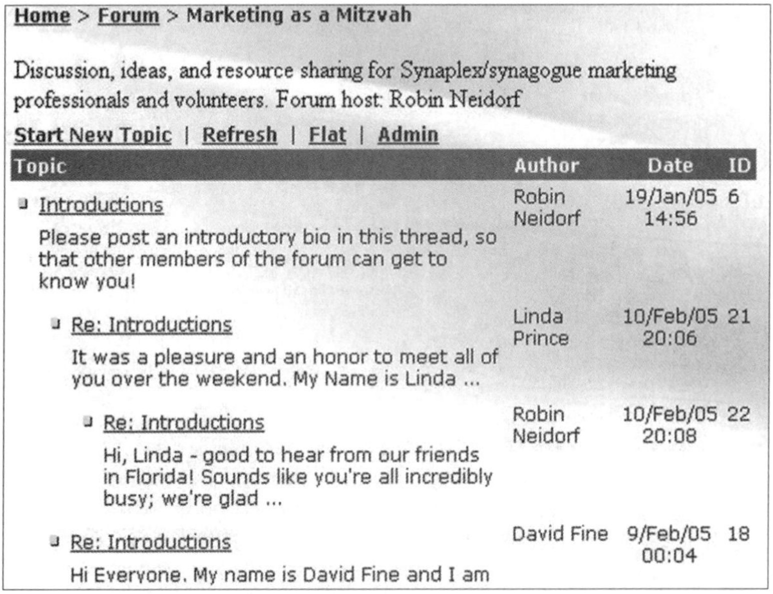

Home > Forum > Marketing as a Mitzvah

Discussion, ideas, and resource sharing for Synaplex/synagogue marketing professionals and volunteers. Forum host: Robin Neidorf

Start New Topic | Refresh | Flat | Admin

Topic	Author	Date	ID
Introductions Please post an introductory bio in this thread, so that other members of the forum can get to know you!	Robin Neidorf	19/Jan/05 14:56	6
Re: Introductions It was a pleasure and an honor to meet all of you over the weekend. My Name is Linda ...	Linda Prince	10/Feb/05 20:06	21
Re: Introductions Hi, Linda - good to hear from our friends in Florida! Sounds like you're all incredibly busy; we're glad ...	Robin Neidorf	10/Feb/05 20:08	22
Re: Introductions Hi Everyone. My name is David Fine and I am	David Fine	9/Feb/05 00:04	18

Figure 1.1 An asynchronous discussion taking place on a bulletin board as part of the Marketing as a Mitzvah program I developed and run for STAR (Synagogues: Transformation and Renewal) (www.starsynagogue.org). The system is a product of UK-based Willco (www.willco.com), which integrates the bulletin board into our database and e-newsletter publishing capabilities.

- **Blog:** Short for "Weblog," creates an online journal or diary of comments, either from a single blogger or from multiple members of a blog group. Unlike other forms of AD, blogs do not create threads (messages grouped by topic) and so are difficult to use for give-and-take among participants.
- **Newsgroup:** Delivers discussion elements directly to users' desktop e-mail system, although the postings themselves are hosted on a remote, secure server (see Figure 1.2).

Does it matter how each type works or which form you are actually using? For the most part, no. Most AD formats follow the same flow of interaction: A comment or question is posted as a new message. A participant can post a response to the message, which all participants will be able to read. Another participant can reply to the original message or to

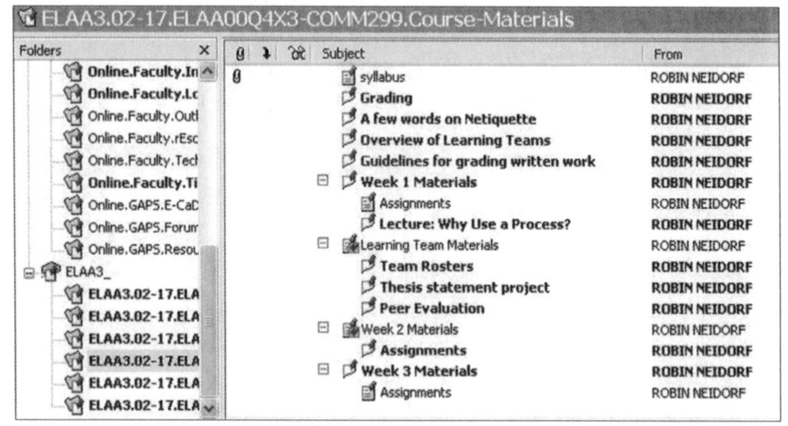

Figure 1.2 My Course Materials newsgroup for a University of Phoenix Online course. Note how materials are organized into easy-to-view threads. Newsgroups operate primarily through Microsoft's Outlook Express e-mail software, although they can also be accessed from a university's secure Web site, if need be. Changing the properties of the display allows me to sort discussions by contributor, date, or subject line, as well as search the newsgroup for keywords—very handy features to use when I'm grading classroom participation!

the response, and so on. The entire discussion appears as indented entries, one after another, under the main thread established by the first posting. (Blogs are the exception in that, as previously noted, they have no threads.) The result is access to the interactions and activity of the classroom anytime, anywhere.

AD is a critical component of many online forms of distance learning because of the immense benefits it offers both students and instructors—benefits that cannot be matched in the face-to-face classroom, in fact. Although many traditional classrooms rely on discussion to deepen the learning of participants and share information, the potential for thoughtful contribution from diverse groups of students is far greater in online AD because it

- Benefits students who tend to hang back in face-to-face discussions, preferring to think through their responses before jumping in

- Benefits students who tend to learn through reading rather than through listening
- Offers greater flexibility to students, which contributes to the diversity in the classroom (as an instructor, I find this diversity to be particularly stimulating because it brings my own thinking to places I never expected to go)
- Enables simultaneous discussions on multiple topics, adding to the richness and depth of the dialogue
- Automatically archives all contributions for later review (making it easier for instructors to grade on the basis of what actually took place rather than their recollection of what took place) and allows data to be searched and sorted by date, contributor, topic, etc.

If AD represents the potential of online distance learning tools, it also highlights many of their weaknesses, including:

- **Lack of immediacy.** This is a recurring theme because it's often a source of anxiety and dissatisfaction for participants in distance learning. Waiting 24 hours for a response to a contribution in a discussion can dampen the spark of your intellectual excitement.
- **Emphasis on written communication skills.** Frequent typos, ignorance of grammar rules, flat-footed attempts at humor that turn into gross interpersonal misunderstandings—you'll see them all in ADs, and from both novice and experienced users.

Despite the challenges of AD, it is an invaluable tool for distance learning. For me, and for most of the distance-learning instructors I know, incorporating AD into a new program isn't a decision, it's a given.

Videoconference

In a videoconference, remote sites are linked via satellite. A camera and screen are set up in each remote location, and participants can see and respond directly to one another by talking to the camera and watching each other on the screen. Any number of remote sites can be linked together, although more than four or five can be cumbersome

A Quick View of Asynchronous Discussion

Pros: Widely accepted; you are likely to have students with experience in asynchronous discussion (AD). Easy to incorporate into a system with other features or as part of a comprehensive course management system. Appropriate for all levels and all topics of study. Has low-cost options and is often included with a larger package.

Cons: Some learning curve at first, to understand how best to use AD and respond effectively and efficiently. A busy class can mean a lot of reading and responding. You may find yourself acting as a de facto writing and communication coach in addition to teaching your actual subject. (And if your own typing or writing skills need work, well, there are a number of distance-learning courses to help you improve them.)

Works best for: In-depth discussion among multiple students; group dialogue.

Messages it sends: Convenience and flexibility; text matters, and e-neatness counts.

and confusing. Many students can participate at each location, enabling large classes to convene despite great distances.

Two years ago, I fielded many more questions about videoconferencing than I do today. With the growth of Web-based conferencing (see "Most-Complex Tools" to follow), the challenges of videoconferencing no longer seem worth the effort to overcome. The equipment is expensive, and fully functional videoconference suites are costly to rent on a regular basis. If many participants are joining the videoconference from several locations, they need to coordinate schedules, room availability, space, and seating. The technology is limited: The classroom has a kind of "talking heads" quality because body language and nuances of expression are not captured and transmitted. Transmission delays and dissonance between speech and movement can also be difficult to follow.

A Quick View of Videoconferencing

Pros: Can approximate the visual and audio stimulation of a classroom; enables far-flung groups to see and hear one another in a synchronous environment.
Cons: Coordinating locations and times can be challenging logistically; equipment is very expensive, so most instructors will need to find a service provider with videoconference suites. Time delays and poor picture quality can negatively impact the overall experience.
Works best for: Groups that are already used to working via video conference; programs that need only one or two conference sessions to be successful; launch or climax of a program, when the special-event element of the conference will complement the occasion.
Messages it sends: High-tech can also be personal; awkward connection is better than none at all.

However, a videoconference is still a viable option if the circumstances are appropriate. Companies that specialize in virtual offices, like HQ Global Workplaces (www.hq.com), make videoconference suites available on an hourly basis, as do select locations of FedEx Kinkos (www.kinkos.com). As long as all the participants have access to a provider, the conference can easily take place.

Most-Complex Tools

You need budget, support, and knowledgeable partners to use the most complex tools of distance instruction to their potential. These are all tools with fairly steep learning curves for you as an instructor and often for your students as well. You will have to be open and creative in how you use them, and you must work well with your team to develop and implement great learning experiences with them. Keep in mind that your students may also need more training to use these tools than they will with less complex options—something to consider when thinking about who your students are or will be and how ready they are to leap into a technology-rich environment.

Multimedia

Pop a CD into a desktop computer and go in-depth with video and audio clips, computer simulations, interactive tools, resources, and more. A multimedia component of a distance-learning program can be a kind of über-textbook, incorporating all the whiz-bang Information Age elements that plain, flat paper can never compete with—including easy searching ("I know it's in here somewhere . . . on page 300? No, on page 525?").

Multimedia has so many potential applications and uses that it would be impossible to list them all. Searchable video and audio clips, simulations, "game" approaches to learning problems, custom-built software—multimedia is limited only by your instructional imagination, the skill of your developers, and your budget.

Multimedia can be created as a stand-alone component—distributed via CD or DVD—or integrated into a Web-based approach.

Proprietary Web Course Management System

Web-based learning is hot, hot, hot, but it's not easy to untangle the various features, quirks, plusses, and minuses of the various packages available. On a recent visit to Edutools (www.edutools.info), an online clearinghouse for information relating to distance-learning tools and best practices, I found reviews of 42 different systems (not including various versions of systems), as well as another 22 systems that were scheduled for review.

A handful of brands have emerged as industry leaders. WebCT and Blackboard, in particular, are the products of choice in universities, businesses, and organizations worldwide. With training and support available, proprietary Web platforms are flexible, comprehensive, time tested, and adaptable to just about any topic or situation. Depending on the kind of access an organization has created, instructors can either upload their own materials or submit materials to a developer, who will then build the classroom environment and test all functions.

A Quick View of Multimedia

Pros: Rich media incorporation, creating a "see, touch, and do" virtual environment. CD/DVD implementations offer portability, detail, and depth without requiring high-speed Internet access. From the student's standpoint, relatively easy to use.

Cons: Expensive to create and update—best for information and material that will have a long shelf life. Still requires baseline technology (a computer that can handle the media or a broadband Internet connection for Web-based programs). Although students can interact with the content itself, they do not interact with an instructor or other students unless other media (e-mail, links to Web-based chat or discussion, opportunity to turn in results, or other response mechanism) are incorporated into the program.

Works best for: Instruction that benefits from simulation; content that will not change anytime soon; high-budget projects.

Messages it sends: High cost, raising expectations of high quality.

Vendors offer systems with unique features designed to solve particular pedagogical problems or cater to the needs of various kinds of learners. For example, Horizon Wimba (www.horizonwimba.com) offers a system specially designed to enhance distance instruction in foreign languages. It includes a speak-and-hear component that allows students to record and play back their attempts at speaking the language. These recordings can be shared with the instructor or simply played back to train the ear to the sounds of the language.

The market for these systems changes at the speed of e-business ("here today, gone tomorrow"). In addition to Edutools, Learning Peaks (www.learningpeaks.com), a site owned and maintained by online-learning consultant Patti Shank, is a good resource for getting a sense of the current state of the industry; other resources can be found at the companion site for this book (www.electric-muse.com/tbyr.asp).

The most common features used in these systems include AD, private journals, electronic attendance and grade books, group functions that enable and enhance teamwork among dispersed students, file sharing, live event capability, e-whiteboard (a shared screen that participants can "write" on with drawing tools and share in real time), lecture postings, links to other resources and readings, and e-library connections. Courses often include in-class e-mail systems or a "digest" feature that allows instructors to collect responses to given discussion topics and distribute them automatically via e-mail to class participants, turning a "pull" communication (one the user has to go out and get) into a "push" communication (one that comes directly to the user). Some vendors also make course content available in the form of a course library that instructors or organizations can access and implement, either off the shelf or with some customizations.

A Quick View of Proprietary Web Course Management System

Pros: Flexibility and just about every feature an instructor could want. High-quality technical and instructional design support; 24/7 access, assuming your connections are reliable.

Cons: Connections aren't always as reliable as they seem. High costs go with high quality and rich features. Steep learning curve for first-time instructors and students (expect a lot of questions that are the electronic equivalent of "Where's the bathroom?"). Material upload may need to take place through an intermediary, adding layers of time and complexity to the work of implementing and revising a course. Without high-speed access, some features are unusable.

Works best for: Instructors with technical support and student support services available to them (or who can contract with the vendor to provide those services).

Messages it sends: High-quality offering, at least equivalent to traditional classrooms; some front-end psychological commitment on the part of the student (no less than the instructor) to learn to use the platform.

And of course, proprietary Web-based classrooms reap the benefits of any Web-based solution: access to other Web-based resources at the click of a mouse.

Open-Source Web-Based Course Management System

With most of the features and benefits of proprietary platforms, open-source systems, such as Jones e-education (www.jones knowledge.com, free to secondary and postsecondary education organizations), Drupal (www.drupal.org), and Moodle (www.moodle.org), are tempting alternatives for any instructor who wants to minimize costs and does not suffer from technophobia. However, these tools lack technical support. If you have a question, you are at the mercy of your peers, who often congregate online in user groups. To be sure, these peer groups can be marvelously generous with ideas and assistance, but remember: You get what you pay for.

Interestingly, there are a growing number of e-learning consultants who specialize in crafting solutions based on open-source systems; visit the Web site for an open-source system like Moodle, and you can find links to consultants who, for a fee, will build a customized solution based on the open-source code.

Still, free is free. Whether you're experimenting with a new idea or playing around with something to see how it might be used, you might find that an open-source program is just the thing.

A Quick View of Open-Source Web-Based Course Management System

Pros: Free, yet feature rich, and with the other benefits of Web-based platforms.

Cons: No technical support, yet the learning curve is just as steep as with any other complex tool.

Works best for: Testing ideas; instructors who are comfortable tinkering with technology.

Messages it sends: Same as proprietary Web-based platform.

Collaborative Online Workspace

Take a secure Web site and fold in IM, e-mail, AD, and Web-based conferencing and presentations. Throw in a dash of blogging and a soupçon of Web publishing capabilities, and—*voila!*—you have a collaborative online workspace. Collaborative Web space consultant David R. Woolley, maintains a comprehensive, annotated list of such tools at his highly informational Web site (www.thinkofit.com), which listed more than 50 different vendors as of May 2005.

It's difficult to visualize a collaborative online workspace without actually visiting and playing with one. Originally designed to enable teamwork among distributed business groups, collaborative online workspaces have been adapted successfully for distance learning, among other applications. An instructor can organize the space to designate core content components, establish team projects, and track assignments and deadlines. Participants can join secure IM sessions, attend real-time online lectures or presentations, and brainstorm together with whiteboard features.

Costs for these systems vary a great deal, depending on the organization you work for and the functions that you appeal to the most. Some hosted solutions charge by the seat, others offer licenses for small and midsize groups, and enterprise editions handle users in the thousands. Still, other systems are free for nonprofit or personal use and may be a good way to test an idea before committing to a long-term solution.

Perhaps the biggest challenge of using a collaborative Web space for an instructional program is that the software was not originally designed to address the particular challenges of instruction. Education-focused solutions such as course management systems were built from the ground up with the needs and interests of instructors and students in mind; collaborative Web space lacks this focus and may need some modifications to get it to behave the way you want.

One example of a successful collaborative online workspace is the Wiki-Wiki Classroom. *Wiki-wiki* is Hawaiian for "quick-quick" (I am *not* making this up!), and a wiki is an open-source Web page that any user can edit or modify at any time. A wiki manager (for instance, an instructor) can set up controls for the people who have access to the wiki, the pages that can be edited and by whom, and the overall design of the pages. In other words, a wiki can be used as a collaborative online workspace and function as a classroom, discussion, workshop, and Web-based publication all at the same time.

It costs nothing other than Web server space to start and maintain a wiki, which makes it an extremely low-cost approach to getting a collaborative workspace for educational purposes. You can get an idea of what a wiki can do by visiting the Wikimedia Foundation (www.wikimediafoundation.org), an international nonprofit company dedicated to using wikis to put the sum of human knowledge into the hands of people around the world.

Wikis and other collaborative online workspaces can be disconcerting for people who are not extremely comfortable with the Web or with technology. They work best for instructors and student populations who are highly savvy about technology.

A Quick View of Collaborative Online Workspace

Pros: Allows many different kinds of interactions and a multiplicity of ways to present and interact with materials; lets instructors create pages and resources on the fly, in partnership with students.

Cons: Steep learning curve for working within the workspace; software not designed with educational applications in mind.

Works best for: Student groups (and instructors) who are very comfortable with technology and visually literate.

Messages it sends: Convenient, tech-intensive, and active classroom; emphasis on collaborative learning experiences. Students will be an active part of creating the space in which learning will take place.

Flexible Combinations—Blended Learning

Any and all of these tools can be part of a distance-learning program. In fact, most of them can also be part of a traditional program. Many traditional classrooms incorporate a Web component, and even middle-school students may be asked to e-mail their assignments. As learning and education continue to evolve, the distinctions between one kind of teaching and another are becoming less and less distinct.

In our own work as instructors (and as students of what it means to be instructors), the keyword is *flexibility*. Evaluate what you want to impart to a group of students, their readiness (and yours) to use various tools, your budget, and your technical resources. Then examine all the options for creating the right combination of interaction, presentation, teamwork, research, creative thinking, response, and feedback. You may find a combination that feels right and comfortable for many kinds of teaching situations, or you may find you need to start from scratch with each course you design. Instructors who are working with institutions that have access to particular tools (such as a license to use a proprietary Web course management system) have an opportunity to experiment with different functions and utilities to see what they like, but may also have to contend with external requirements not of their choosing. (See "What If You Don't Have a Choice?" later in this chapter.)

I've presented the tools of distance learning as if there were bright lines separating one from another. In reality, the boundaries are quite a bit fuzzier. Evolutions and revolutions in telecommunications technology are blurring the borders between teleconference and Webinar, and between AD and a collaborative Web space. My experience with a wide range of students and tools suggests that the readiness factor will dictate the usability of a technology for a given project even more than the functionality of the technology itself.

For example, I regularly work with a group of professionals on nonprofit marketing skills and knowledge. This group is very comfortable with a teleconference but very *un*comfortable with a Web-based conference. My efforts to push members into moving our teleconferences online have been met with enormous resistance. Still, I find ways to incorporate some elements of Web-based communication, such as asking them to be online during our calls so that we can look at the same page at the same time. They are starting to see the possibilities and are developing a greater level of readiness to take the next step.

You have to know your student population and how to introduce tools, train them in usage and interaction, and have the appropriate level of support to ease their fears and troubleshoot the inevitable hiccups that happen at the most inconvenient times. Merging technologies is exciting and creates enormous possibilities for instruction. But developments in technology often outpace our human ability to adjust. There are two things to keep in mind: "focus on function" and the continuum concept. Focus on function tells us to identify what we want to do with a tool or technology and then get advice on the best match for our needs. The continuum concept reminds us that technology moves along a continuum from simple to complex and that human willingness to use technology moves along a continuum from unwilling to enthusiastic. The best pairings of users and technology happen when willingness to use the tools meshes with the complexity of the tool.

Right Tool, Right Place—A Few Sample Approaches

Still having trouble visualizing what your distance-instruction toolkit might look like in practice? Following are a few sample combinations of tools and instructional approaches to help you think of ways to use these tools in various situations.

Low-Tech, Low-Cost Professional Writing Workshop

Description: This is a 3-week workshop for a targeted group of professionals seeking to improve their writing skills.

Tools used: E-mail discussion list, teleconference, private e-mail, and fax exchange.

Approach: The course begins with a teleconference, in which the participants and instructor introduce themselves and discuss their personal goals for the course. The instructor uses the call to lay out the four content areas they will cover with e-mail lectures, e-mail discussions, and peer-to-peer mentoring work. Following the call, the instructor e-mails the first lecture and assignments. The participants discuss the topics via e-mail, and then e-mail their first assignment to the instructor. The instructor makes detailed notes on the assignments and e-mails them back. (One student has trouble viewing the comments; the instructor faxes a copy of the marked-up document for her review.)

Throughout the course, the instructor monitors discussions and directs students toward additional resources for in-depth learning. New topics are introduced with e-mailed lectures and assignments. The participants also work in pairs to review and edit each other's work. A second conference call allows the instructor to pull together the threads of activity and direct participants on a final project. Final projects are e-mailed to the instructor as well as to the entire group.

Introduction to Marketing for Small and Micro-Businesses

Description: Small-business owners and one-person operations take part in a 6-week workshop on marketing strategy and tactics.

Tools used: E-mail, secure online forum with digest features, teleconference, and IM.

Approach: Following a launch meeting via teleconference, the participants interact primarily through a Web-based private forum. The instructor posts threads within the forum for personal introductions, discussion topics, and questions. Lectures on core topics are posted to the forum and also e-mailed to participants to ensure receipt and review. Participants discuss the lecture and assignments within the forum; every day, the forum software automatically creates a daily summary document—a digest—and e-mails it to all participants.

Participants also e-mail and call the instructor with individual questions as necessary. They complete a team project by meeting via IM every few days; an archive of each IM session is copied into the forum for later reference and review.

Because the forum is Web-based, the instructor is able to incorporate live links to other Web sites, an online collection of business references, and other resources. One assignment involves sending the participants to several of these resources to conduct specific research tasks.

The teams present their final projects both online in the forum and via teleconference. Before the teleconference, each team e-mails its presentation and handouts to all the other participants. During the teleconference, all participants have the presentations in front of them (either on the screen or in a printout), and they use each presentation as a visual reference.

Leadership Development Program

Description: This is a rigorous, 8-week seminar on leadership and management skills for rabbis who are 2 to 5 years past their ordination and serving full-time in a pulpit.

Tools: Proprietary Web platform, DVD, teleconference, and e-mail.

Approach: Before the launch of the course, participants and the instructor join a teleconference orientation session, in which the course developer demonstrates all the features and tools of the course. Participants have an opportunity to log in, find assignments, review resources, and post messages to the AD forum. A DVD containing live interviews with noted rabbis is mailed to participants before the start of the course. Course content refers to these interviews, which participants can play, search, and save clips from. They can also view, search, and print a text transcript. Once class begins, all participation takes place within the secure course site. Students can review resources, take online quizzes, participate in discussion, post their thoughts to a private journal, and turn in assignments to the instructor's "drop box." They also contact the instructor privately via e-mail or phone as necessary.

Student-Led Creative Writing Workshop

Description: Although this course involves an instructor, it is largely driven by the students participating. This course is an ongoing writing workshop in which students are reading and commenting on literature while working on their own poems and stories.

Tools: Collaborative Web space.

Approach: Students join the course on an ongoing basis, so there is no launch per se. As they join, they are invited to create their own links from the course's home page to post original work. They can comment on each other's work by visiting a classmate's page and adding a comment to that page's blog, which functions like an open diary available to anyone who wants to contribute. An AD board hosts their reviews and analysis of the literary works they are studying. The instructor posts new assignments and readings once a month and monitors all activity to ensure the students are participating and adhering to the loose rules of the classroom.

Another page within the collaborative Web space collects ideas for submissions to literary journals and other publishers; students can add to and edit this page on the fly, adding live links to journal Web sites, thereby creating their own private library of submission guidelines.

As you can see, the combinations are limited only by your creativity, your (and your students') willingness to use the tools, and your budget. Of course, willingness and budget may be significant limitations, but the important thing to recognize is that the functionality to make just about any distance-learning program succeed is available. There are solutions for any kind of instructional needs if you are willing to experiment and work with your students and support teams to explore their potential.

Distance-Learning Tools—Do's and Don'ts

Do:

Ask informed questions.

Demo a tool before you commit to using it.

Try freeware or open-source tools (but keep in mind the caveats discussed in the text).

Go for low tech whenever possible.

Ask potential students for their input.

Network with other instructors; ask them what they use; compare notes, success stories, and battle scars.

Keep up with changing technology; treat yourself to an occasional seminar or conference.

Stay open, creative, and flexible about your teaching.

Assume that you *will* find the right solution (although it may not be the one you thought you'd find).

Don't:

Use technology for its own sake; it must enhance the learning and instructing experience or it will be merely distracting (at best) or a barrier (at worst).

Change your requirements, objectives, or audiences without considering their impact on choice of tools.

Change your requirements, objectives, or audiences without keeping your partners (especially your technology partners) informed.

Assume everything will work as promised; test and retest (preferably with members of the learner population) before the course begins.

Ignore the unwillingness of your students to use a tool; sometimes they're just not ready and you may need to take smaller incremental steps than you'd like.

Let failure or challenges discourage you from believing in the possibilities of distance education.

"Get married" to a particular tool or solution; it might not be all things to all situations.

Use the tool as a substitute for good course design and delivery.

Migrate content from one tool to another in a cut-and-paste approach.

What If You Don't Have a Choice?

Sometimes decisions about tools are made without input from those who will need to use them. The good news is that fiats from above are often for enterprisewide solutions that come with all the features you could want or need and often with technical support and consulting assistance to help users access those features. Still, it can be a challenge to hook up your donkey to an elephant harness, and technical support isn't always all it's touted to be.

If this is your situation now or in the future, you may be in for a real (ahem) learning experience—in the best sense, of course! First of all, adaptation to a required tool or protocol can open up your teaching in an entirely new way, forcing you to examine why you approach teaching the way you do and pushing you toward greater creativity as an instructor.

Self-examination aside, it's almost always possible to make a solution work (after all, isn't that what solutions are supposed to do?), if the technology is sound. You might find it helpful to complete the work described in Chapters 3 and 4 on prepping your course, then share the results with a development specialist whose job is to help instructors use the designated system. Depending on the requirements and complexity of the work involved, you may even want to work directly with an instructional designer who specializes in distance learning or the system you plan on using.

Remember that you can always add a stand-alone component to an existing system. For instance, you might add Web-based real-time collaboration or conferencing to an otherwise asynchronous environment. Having a comprehensive sense of the available technology can be very helpful in such a case: If the established tool isn't doing something you need it to do, à la carte options can turn something clunky into something quite elegant.

Bottom line: Keep an open mind, once you get a good rant out of your system about the clueless decision makers who couldn't teach a spider to spin a web. At its best, being an instructor means being a perpetual learner.

A View into the Future

Much of distance learning consists of building on the technological developments that are taking place all around us. What's possible today may have only been a vision 5 years ago, and the evolution is only accelerating. I can't see the future in a crystal ball, but I can offer a perspective on what to watch for.

Ease of Use

Tools are becoming more user friendly with every iteration. Next-generation tools will be more intuitive and continue the trend toward graphic-driven interfaces that look and feel like the software and systems that users are already familiar with.

Deeper Integration

As evolution in technology continues, the boundaries between one type of tool and another will continue to be blurred and even erased. At the same time, technology tools will become a more seamless part of the educational experience; most courses will find ways to deepen the learning experience by integrating tools like Web-based collaboration, AD, and listservs into the standard curriculum.

Shorter Learning Curve for New Students

The pool of adults who have already participated in some form of distance learning is growing all the time; even those who have not participated in distance learning are gaining more experience with the technology that distance learning uses. As we all gain more experience, the learning curve will become less daunting for new students. They will be adapting existing knowledge rather than starting over with something brand new.

At the same time, the youngest generation of adults participating in distance learning will become more present in more classrooms. This generation, which is extremely tech savvy, is very comfortable experimenting with tools and getting them to work. As more members of this generation pursue educational opportunities, they will push their instructors to explore even more potential directions for their learning experience.

Palmtop Applications

Many of the distance tools that rely on technology involve the use of a desktop computer with Internet access. The future of telecommunication, however, is right in the palm of our hands. Innovations in distance learning will create platforms and systems that can be accessed via small mobile units—cellphones, personal digital assistants (PDAs), e-book readers, and the like. Design and functionality will have to undergo some critical rethinking to make the leap.

Just-in-Time Learning

Here is where instruction will start to merge with knowledge management (KM); businesses in particular are looking for learning solutions that deliver the right educational experiences at the moment they are needed and in the most useful format. Course management systems can be tied into knowledge management database systems. If KM systems are populated with targeted learning modules, and if those modules can be accessed and uploaded to a course delivery tool in response to a user's query, quite a few enterprises would be mightily satisfied by the result.

Voice-Over-Internet and Other Merging Technologies

Online classrooms will soon enjoy the richer environment made possible through merging technologies: voice-over-Internet, movie streaming, Web cams that transmit high-quality images very affordably, and more. The tools are moving closer together, becoming less expensive, and passing through the ranks of the early adopters to reach the mainstream.

Eventually, the choice of tools will not be as befuddling as it might seem today. As our expectations of education shift to accept distance models as part of the norm, we'll be able to choose among tools much more easily, even unconsciously, the way we now choose whether to pick up the phone, send an e-mail, or transmit an IM. Ten years ago, sending an e-mail (especially with an attachment!) was a project; I usually had to call recipients to be sure they received the message and were able to read it. Today, I barely notice I'm choosing one communication tool over another. One day, we'll feel similarly about choosing tools for distance instruction.

Worksheet 1.1 on the following pages will help you organize your thoughts about choosing distance learning tools. Visit www.electric-muse.com/tbyr.asp for a Web-based version of this and other worksheets and planning tools.

Worksheet 1.1 Needs and Readiness for Distance-Learning Tools

Use this worksheet to help determine what you may need in a distance-learning tool and how ready you may be for technology.

1. Budget

Do you know your budget for a distance-learning tool? Y/N

Budget is approximately: __________ per course
semester
year
student
other: ______________

What factors influence the budget?

2. Functional Needs

Which of these functions does your distance-learning program require?

Functions—Communication and Classroom	**No Need**	**Could Use**	**Must Have**	**Don't Know**
E-mail				
Asynchronous discussion				
Synchronous discussion/IM				
Teleconference				
Webinar				
Web-based collaborative space				
Online whiteboard				
Blog				
Voice over Internet				
Video over Internet				
Video conferencing				
Multimedia (Web based)				
Multimedia (CD/DVD-based)				
Custom applications				
Other:				
Other:				
Other:				

Worksheet 1.1 (cont.)

Functions—Administrative	**No Need**	**Could Use**	**Must Have**	**Don't Know**
Electronic gradebook				
Attendance				
Usage monitoring				
Secure payment				
Secure registration				
Student records access				
Instructor access to course controls				
Scalability				
Other:				
Other:				

Of the functions you have listed as "must have," which are your highest priority?

What systems or tools have you used, demo'd, or observed in action?

Please rate your agreement with the following statements, where 1 = completely disagree and 5 = completely agree:

	1	2	3	4	5
I am comfortable learning to use new technology.					
I need to use tools that are extremely easy to get started.					
Budget is the most important factor in my decision about which tools to use.					
It is important that I choose a tool that does not require high-speed Internet access.					
It is important that I not rely too heavily on technology.					
My students are comfortable learning to use new technology.					
My students have access to appropriate technology.					

When you have completed the worksheet, review again the information presented in Chapter 1 to determine which tools are most appropriate for your needs and readiness. Visit www.electric-muse.com/tbyr.asp for a Web-based version of this worksheet that you can adapt to your needs and share with others.

Chapter 2

What to Expect When You're Expecting Students

When I work with business and nonprofit clients on developing an audience-focused approach to their marketing, I hammer one message repeatedly:

It's not about you; it's about *them.*

The most common mistake I see clients make is to create communications that focus on what the company or organization offers. My job is to help them shift their perspective so that their materials put the customer first. It's always about the customers. The material has to speak to them, in their language, and motivate them to deepen their relationship with the company or organization. It has to anticipate and adequately respond to the implicit—or explicit—question: What's in it for me?

A similar shift is necessary for instructors who are used to thinking primarily about what they offer rather than what their students may need. For distance learning to succeed, it has to be about *the students.* In fact, the best educational experiences, distance or otherwise, are those built around what the learner wants, needs, expects, and anticipates.

Under any circumstances, it's a tough challenge to develop and deliver an engaging, effective course focused on student needs and desired outcomes. In distance learning, the challenge is compounded by the broader range of students' skills, interests, backgrounds, and levels of engagement. And, as discussed in Chapter 1, the nuances of media and their uses will have a profound effect on how students encounter and work with the material, the instructor, and each other.

Most instructors intuitively understand how students, individually and as a group, change the entire experience of teaching. After teaching even a handful of classes, you know that every class has its own character. You can teach the same material in the same way over and over again yet create a different learning environment each time because of the human mix. For me and for many of my colleagues, the thrill of this experience is part of the pleasure of teaching. On the flip side, of course, are the disaster classes, in which the chemistry just doesn't work. (They're no fun for anyone involved—students, instructor, or the long-suffering friends who have to hear about them throughout the duration.)

Although you will never have control over some elements of your classroom chemistry, you can create the conditions for success if you understand who your students are (or will be) and what they need, and then use that knowledge to plan and craft learning experiences that will bring out the best in them. You can build this knowledge in two ways. First, use the information in this chapter to develop a baseline understanding of the types of students you are likely to encounter, in terms of their expectations, learning styles, and how they will interact with you, each other, and the material. Second, identify the kinds of students—their characteristics and needs—you want to be working with and market your offerings specifically to attract them. (For ideas and resources relating to marketing your distance-instruction offerings, visit the companion site for this book: www.electric-muse.com/tbyr.asp.)

Understanding Adult Learners

This chapter—and this book—assumes that you will be working with adult students. They may be nontraditional college students, professionals seeking development and training, association members gaining industry knowledge, or leisure-time students pursuing personal enrichment opportunities. They may be on the cusp of adulthood, in their late teens or early 20s; they may be enhancing their retirement years with learning in new areas. Distance-learning students will come to you with all kinds of skills, experiences, backgrounds, and history as learners. I've worked with relatively recent immigrants from Asia and Latin America in the same class with second- or third-career learners pursuing a new line of work. When teaching through the University of Phoenix Online, I often facilitate courses made up entirely of active-duty members of the military at various stages of their careers and stationed throughout the world.

Despite the diversity, these groups of learners have some things in common. It's important for instructors to understand five key characteristics shared by most adult learners.

First Key Characteristic: Personal History and Experience

Adult learners are not blank slates. They come into the classroom with the wisdom of experience. They have a personal history of and relationship with their own identity as students: Some loved school and excelled in every endeavor, whereas others have more ambivalent feelings about formal education. Most have some professional experience, which has a deep impact on what they want to learn and why. At the same time, they have a variety of interpersonal experiences, which impact how they interact with classmates as well as instructors. With adult learners, you get the whole package.

In a distance-learning context, adult learners also bring their history (or lack thereof) with distance education. Some may have experienced distance education, and they will bring into your classroom certain expectations of what the experience should be like. Your requirements and approach may come as a surprise to them (hopefully, a good surprise). I've found that even at the University of Phoenix Online, where instructors are trained to very specific program requirements, my students are frequently surprised by the approach I take in guiding them through the course. "My last instructor never ..." and "My last instructor always ..." are comments I hear all too often.

Of course, you may also have students with no experience in a distance-learning environment, and they too will come with assumptions and expectations about what it will be like. Often students expect their first distance-learning experience to be relatively lightweight compared with traditional classes. (In my distance-learning programs, they are soon disabused of that notion!)

Instructors need to take into account the way personal history and experience will color the perspective of their adult students. Most of all, we need to respect the life wisdom of these students and find ways to honor and validate that wisdom through our courses.

Second Key Characteristic: Preferred Learning Style

Every human has a preferred way to encounter and master new information. Some are audio learners who absorb information best when they can hear it; others are textual learners who prefer the written word; still others are hands-on learners who need a lab course to get their brains fully engaged with the material. A basic understanding of learning styles is critical to being successful as a distance instructor. (It doesn't hurt in any kind of instructional situation, actually—including parenting!)

Later in this chapter, we'll explore learning styles in greater detail, including how to identify and teach these styles.

Third Key Characteristic: Additional Responsibilities and Demands on Their Time

Have you noticed that your adult students are often running just a little bit late, are suddenly out of commission because a family member is sick, or seem to be distracted by managing the details of their lives? The pace of most of our lives outruns our ability to keep up. Busy adults who are also pursuing an education require instructors who understand the demands on their time. This doesn't mean accepting wholesale excuses for late or missing work, slapdash participation, or other kinds of sloughing off. It does mean, however, that an instructor might want to consider carefully the appropriate workload, time frame, or technology for a course. For instance, the fact that I work with busy adults (and that I am one myself) is one of the reasons I almost always incorporate an asynchronous discussion (AD) component into my distance offerings. When I train students in the appropriate use of AD, the tool enables us to create a deeply collaborative environment for discussion and exchange without requiring us to be anywhere at the same time. The flexibility of the tool is well adapted to the needs of busy adults.

When I first plan a class, I'm also careful to consider how much my students will be able to accomplish in a particular time frame. I often find myself pulling back on the breadth of material I want to cover in favor of creating more in-depth learning on a narrower topic. Covering smaller chunks in greater depth enables me to deliver courses that require shorter time commitments of my students while helping them achieve meaningful results. Translation: ongoing and deepened motivation through incremental success.

Fourth Key Characteristic: Variety of Motivations to Learn

Yet another key characteristic of adult students is that they seek out and participate in educational experiences for unique reasons. They look to learning to satisfy a broad range of needs and interests.

Understanding and capitalizing on an individual's motivation to learn are mission-critical skills for a distance instructor. We'll discuss in greater detail how to leverage student motivation later in this chapter and in more detail in Chapter 6. For now, just keep in mind that students' motivations will tell you plenty about how to work with them. Every interaction between you and the student needs to push the student's motivational buttons.

Fifth Key Characteristic: Psychological Dimensions

Finally, adult students arrive in our classrooms with their egos, fears, and defense mechanisms in working order. Even students who seem incredibly confident and competent may be harboring (or compensating for) secret fears about their ability to succeed.

No one likes to feel like a beginner, and adult students may be returning to formal learning after a long hiatus. The added uncertainties of distance learning—for students who are used to traditional classrooms—can inhibit performance even more. Distance instructors working with adults need to help students feel confident and capable even as they introduce new ideas and skills.

Unlike children, who are wired to learn, many adults find learning to be a scary experience. After all, learning means change. Learning also means admitting one's own deficiencies. As a distance instructor, it's important to make room for the fears consciously or unconsciously motivating students. Always work on activating and projecting your own sense of empathy, subtly telling students that it's acceptable to feel whatever they're feeling.

Attitudes Toward Education

If adult students share some general characteristics, they are also confoundedly individual. From overall attitudes toward learning, to preferred learning style, to generational differences and more, each student will come to you as a unique blend of unpredictable ingredients. Their variability is one of the reasons instructor-led experiences will always have a preferred place among educational models; the computers can't quite take over our jobs yet!

Confidence Strength Training

One example of confidence building within the context of course work is a regular feature of my writing and composition courses. Students in these classes often come to me with deep anxieties about their ability to write; they've been told by other teachers and even at times by their parents that they are terrible writers. If I ignored the psychological baggage they bring into the classroom with them, I'd never get them to write anything! My strategy, then, is to start by helping them reflect (in writing) on a positive experience they have had with writing—perhaps a love letter or that one assignment that seemed to flow without effort. Throughout the course, even while I'm pushing them to practice difficult skills, I refer back to their positive experiences, pointing out how they are building on abilities they had never recognized in themselves before. By the end of the course, most of the students don't exactly love writing, but at least the disabling anxiety has been neutralized.

Beyond the shared general characteristics of adult students, I've found that there are two kinds of people in this world: perpetual students and outcome-oriented learners.

Perpetual learners may have several academic degrees, a long list of continuing-education credits, and a constant hunger for discovering the next intellectual mountain to climb. They can be challenging students because they demand a lot of satisfaction from their educational experiences. At the same time, they are highly rewarding students to work with because they need just a little light and fertilization to grow like kudzu. For these students, a good instructor is truly a mentor and guide along a path that they are bound and determined to follow. Perpetual learners often thrive on theory and are endlessly enthusiastic about discussion, exploration, dialogue, and debate.

The other type, which has turned up more frequently in my own distance courses, is the outcome-oriented learner. The outcome-oriented learner is pursuing an educational opportunity because of a perceived immediate payback, for example, acquisition of new skills, which can translate into better on-the-job experiences, higher pay, promotion, entry into a new field, and so on. This kind of student wants to know that the time and resources spent mastering the material will result in the expected payoff. For these students, a good instructor lays out a clear path from point A to point B and draws explicit links between any theoretical components of a course and their practical applications. "Trust me; you'll be glad you learned this" is not an effective instructional technique for outcome-oriented learners, who may even be skeptical about the value of education except within the context of their immediate goals.

Of course, there are two other kinds of people in this world: those who think there are two kinds of people in this world, and those who know better. The perpetual learner and the outcome-oriented learner are flat stereotypes—images reproduced with the contrast set way too high, eliminating the texture and character of the real individuals who turn up in our classrooms. If you have an opportunity to work with a group of learners over a period of time, you will likely discover that the boundaries between these two types are rather more permeable than otherwise. Outcome-oriented learners may discover a latent love of theory and debate, while perpetual students, when bored or (worse) disappointed, may simply want to cut to the practical details in a course and move on.

Why present these types at all if they are such a poor representation of reality? Because, as types, they can help you form an introductory understanding of the kinds of students you may be working with and the kind of student you may be.

I am a perpetual learner; I'd be happy to pursue degree after degree for the sheer joy of it. (My family is grateful that responsibilities such as earning a living preclude the fulfillment of that particular dream.) However, the large majority of the students I work with in professional development and in undergraduate degree programs are outcome-oriented learners. They have a particular personal goal in mind that usually involves advancement and improved professional skills rather than the content of my course per se, let alone the joy of learning. Through the process of trial and error, I figured out why the things that naturally motivated me were not working to motivate my students. I couldn't figure out why they weren't jumping into the online discussion and batting ideas back and forth since that's what *I* would do. I had an inkling of why they were unwilling to slog through theoretical readings that underlay the assignments, but I was absolutely baffled by their *refusal* to do so when the theory was so important to the work.

And then, after months of frustration, I started to realize something: I had to motivate outcome-oriented learners on *their* terms to do what I wanted them to do. I had to be sure to make theoretical readings as grounded in practical reality as possible. I couldn't assume that once they read the material, they would figure out the link, and I couldn't assume that they would even read the material simply because it was assigned.

With that insight, I shifted the way I designed my courses and laid out assignments. I rewrote most of my syllabi and lectures to motivate students in different ways. In creating assignments, I began to offer choices that would help perpetual learners come down to earth and push outcome-oriented learners toward a more systemic understanding of the material.

Know the kind of learners you are working with and craft your approach to hit *their* points of motivation.

Learning Styles

Most of us, through elementary school, high school, and even college or postgraduate studies, encountered little understanding or nurturing of our personal learning style. Whether we preferred to learn verbally or visually, kinetically or collaboratively, we sat in classrooms, listened to lectures, occasionally worked on team projects, researched and wrote papers, participated in lab sections, and more or less sank or swam, based on how well we adapted and responded to presentational education.

The science of understanding how humans absorb information and turn it into competence has come a long way in the past few decades. Many of these insights have already found their way into classrooms of all kinds—certainly, our culture's nascent understanding of multiple intelligences is beginning to achieve a certain household word status—but many of us who are now instructors were ourselves educated in a system blind to learning styles. As a result, our unconscious models of what it means to teach do not reflect important insights into learning styles and how to work with them.

The research on learning styles indicates that styles are not static; most of us can accommodate educational situations that do not speak to our preferred style as long as we can use our preferred style some of the time.

Unfortunately, unique styles are difficult to accommodate in a traditional face-to-face classroom.

One of the great benefits of distance learning is that it is easier for an instructor to help students customize the experience based on the preferences of the learner; thus, each learner can satisfy the needs of his or her preferred learning style more frequently than in the traditional classroom. An audio learner can access material in ways that maximize these learning strengths, while a textual learner has options more suited to a reading-and-absorption style.

Most of all, distance learning permits repetition of concepts or exercises that are particularly challenging, allowing learners to customize their experience even further. Students can review and repeat to master the areas of study they most need to work on, while moving quickly through (or even testing out of) areas of study they have already mastered.

Three's the Charm

Throughout this book, you'll find a lot of emphasis on repetition. Instruction would be much easier if people naturally remembered everything they encountered the first time they encountered it. Unfortunately, our brains do not absorb facts perfectly on first exposure. Some students will remember everything on one exposure; a larger portion of students will remember most information after two exposures; and after three exposures, most students will remember most of the material. That's the rule of three.

The importance of repetition will come up again when we examine the craft of course materials in Chapter 4, as well as in the discussion of classroom management in Chapter 5.

Know Thy Style

What do you know about your own preferred learning style? It might tell you something about your unconscious expectations of what it means to learn. Just as I had to learn that not everyone was a perpetual student, I also had to learn that not everyone shared my preferred learning style.

There are a number of free, Web-based tools that can help you identify and understand your learning style. Here's one to try, just for fun and a bit of insight: www.learning-styles-online.com/inventory measures a user's learning preferences in seven areas and presents results as a visual graph (see Figure 2.1).

Interesting, huh? I've been asking students to complete one of these self-assessments and e-mail me the results as part of the introductory stages of a course. The students are often intrigued by the way a learning style assessment identifies their strengths and weaknesses, providing information that can help them succeed in my course and others. And as an instructor, I find the results of these assessments to be extremely helpful in getting to know the students and the ways I can best help them achieve their goals.

How to Work with Learning Styles

Entire academic careers have been built on the understanding of learning styles. This is a brief introduction to instructional considerations when working with different styles; you'll want to select materials and options that address different styles so that you can keep your students as engaged as much as possible and allow them to learn effectively.

Verbal Style

Students with a verbal learning style respond to written and spoken language. They will have no trouble absorbing your carefully crafted written lectures or reviewing assignments presented to them in writing. You can maximize their use of distance-learning tools and resources by adding elements such as a glossary, a verbal analysis of concepts, and even word games.

Visual Style

Students with a visual learning style respond to pictures and images. Add to their experience in your distance program by presenting information in the form of mind maps; link concepts to each other on the mind map, or use mind maps to illustrate links between concepts and desired practical outcomes. Virtual whiteboard sessions are great fun for visual learners, who can watch ideas emerge on the screen and even contribute to their

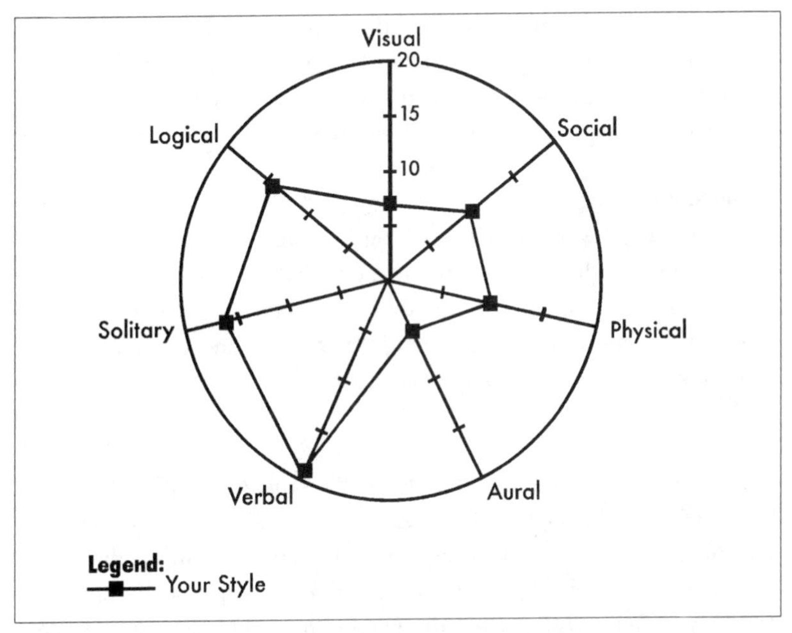

Figure 2.1 The graphical representation of my own learning style, based on the inventory at www.learning-styles-online.com. Don't put me on a learning team or ask me to repeat what I just heard. But if you give me text to analyze on my own, I'll happily get to work. *(Image used with permission of Memletics, Inc., owner of www.learning-styles-online.com. Further information and tools are available at www.memletics.com.)*

creation. Well-designed Web-based learning environments are great for visual students. You can enhance their understanding of key texts by marking them iconographically, for example, placing icons next to particular kinds of text so that these students can visually tell the difference between a definition, an assignment, a team project, and so forth.

Kinesthetic Style

Kinesthetic learners like to "touch and do." This might seem like a difficult style to accommodate in a distance program, but kinesthetic learners can do very well if they are given options that speak to them. Offer projects and assignments that invite them to build a model, draw or construct something, or observe changes in their own physical state while doing an activity. Anything that gets them moving will help them master the material you are presenting. Since kinesthetic learners are often primarily interested in personally experiencing an activity, computer simulations can also be good learning tools for them.

Social Style

Social learners want to do everything in groups. They will be active participants in your distance classroom and with their classmates once they get the hang of how to do it. In addition to team projects, role-playing exercises and group problem-solving assignments are some of the tools you can employ that stimulate social learners.

Solitary Style

Students with a solitary learning style resent team assignments and need to feel confident that they aren't wasting their time with the team. They prefer to go off on their own to learn material. Many of them mistakenly believe that distance learning will mean little social interaction and are painfully surprised to learn that they must interact to succeed. You can help the solitary learner by incorporating several elements into your course: Return regularly to the personal motivation of solitary learners so that they remain committed to the course. Role-playing exercises can also be effective for solitary learners because they can take on someone else's persona for the duration of the project and distance their solitary nature from the immediate learning experience. Having a personal, private course journal for reflection can also help solitary learners interact with the material in a way that honors their learning style while providing you with enough information to help these students make greater progress toward their goals.

Logical Style

The logical learner thrives on reasoning and systems. Logical learners are forever making lists and agendas; they can be a bit annoying on learning teams, but they do help keep things on track. Stimulate logical learners by answering their constant query, "But *why*?" Provide deeper resources, readings, and exercises, beyond the ones you assign for the course, to allow them to dive into the why's as much as they want. Simulations that enable them to test theories and work on a whole system rather than a single piece of it are great fun for logical learners.

Aural Style

The aural learning style is one in which the student responds best to sounds, rhythms, and repetition. Aural students often make up little rhymes to help themselves remember key information. Recorded materials, well-organized telephone calls, and even materials that integrate poetry and rhythmic language can help aural learners interact more intimately with the course.

Balancing Stylistic Needs

If you were to create style-specific pathways through every single course you created, you'd be so busy creating that you'd never have time to teach! The goal should be to offer at least some options some of the time that will appeal to a variety of learning styles. When I create a course, I never have trouble appealing to the verbal or logical styles because I share many of their characteristics. However, I have difficulty thinking through offerings for kinesthetic and social learners; I've made it a point to put those options on my own "course review" checklist to remind myself to create options for them before launching a course.

The need to balance learning styles is another reason that creating distance-learning courses in collaboration with others is so helpful. In a collaborative process, you are sure to be working with individuals who have different learning styles. Use their ideas and input to ensure you are creating materials that will stimulate the widest range of your potential students.

Generational Differences

Advances in healthcare and the trend toward longer professional careers have created an environment in which four distinct generations are active, working, and learning together. The characteristics of today's 18- to 25-year-olds are very different from the characteristics of Generation X, the omnipresent Baby Boomers, and the Matures, who are still in the workforce and may be pursuing distance learning for professional or personal reasons.

As a distance instructor, you may work with students in any and all of the four generations, each of which has its own characteristics, perspectives, and expectations of the classroom environment (see Table 2.1).

Matures

Matures are those born before 1946. The world events that have shaped their lives include World War II, the Korean Conflict, the Depression, and the New Deal. Matures grew up in a world where expectations and roles were clearly defined and values like thrift, hard work, and respect for authority were givens.

As students, Matures may need more time to acclimate to a new environment, regardless of the level of technology involved; they have decades of expectations about what a classroom is like, and most distance-learning programs will upset those expectations.

The importance of peer-to-peer connections may also be challenging for Matures. This is a generation accustomed to well-defined hierarchies. The idea that they are co-creating the learning experience may be a strange one at first.

Another consideration if your learning program will include Matures: larger fonts.

Boomers

What hasn't been written or said about the ubiquitous Baby Boomers? Boomers were born between 1946 and 1964; their childhood and adolescent years were characterized by confidence, prosperity, the rise of youth culture, and growing experimentation with alternative perspectives. A few of the key events shaping Boomers' worldview include the Cuban missile crisis, the Kennedy and King assassinations, and the sexual revolution.

As students, Boomers are often process oriented and committed to building consensus. They can be extremely uncomfortable with open conflict. They are highly team oriented and may be pleasantly surprised at the degree of interaction and kinds of relationships they can develop in a distance-learning environment.

Boomers look to their peers for approval and direction. A bit of positive peer pressure in the motivation department can be very effective in keeping them involved in a course.

Boomers in general want to have a clear idea of what they need to do to succeed; they are deeply committed to their own excellence.

Table 2.1 Know Your Generations

Generation	Life-Defining Events	Core Values	Expectations of Classroom
Matures	WW2 Korean War	Dedication Conformity Respect for authority Adhere to rules Self-sacrifice	Clear hierarchy
Boomers	Civil Rights Women's Lib Cold War	Optimism Team-oriented Manipulation of rules "Live to work"	Discussion and creation of consensus
Generation X	AIDS Persian Gulf Latchkey kids Computers	Diversity Balance Self-reliance "Work to live"	Unimpressed with nominal authority; assign authority based on competence
Millennials	Oklahoma City bombing Columbine shootings Multicultural terrorism Internet	Optimism Civic duty Diversity "Edu-tainment" Collective action	Will cut-and-paste to create customized experience; technology is an enhancement to the process

Adapted from "Higher Education, Blended Learning and the Generations: Knowledge is Power—No More," by Charles Dziuban, Patsy Moskal and Joel Hartman, Research Initiative for Teaching Effectiveness, University of Central Florida and Generations at Work: Managing the Clash of Veterans, Boomers, Xers, and Nexters in Your Workplaces, *by Ron Zemke, Claire Raines, and Bob Filipczak, Amacom, 2000.*

Generation X

Generation X, born between 1965 and 1980, is the first generation to have grown up in a largely technological environment (although the impact is even more profound for the next generation). Critical events in the Generation X lifetime include the Challenger disaster, the spread of AIDS, recession, and massive layoffs.

As students, Gen Xers are cynical about authority, jealous of demands on their time, and committed to finding their own way through the material. Give them lots of options and help them feel you respect their individuality, creativity, and ideas.

Gen Xers are the first generation to grow up with the expectation that they would not have a single lifelong career. They do not expect institutions—or even their own communities—to look after them. Somewhere in the motivational system of most Gen Xers is the sense that education, skills, and even personal enrichment pursuits could pave the way for the next phase of their multistage careers.

Millennials

The Millennials are the youngest generation currently in the workforce and in higher education. Born between 1981 and 1994, Millennials are fully digital and expect organizations to make technology available as a matter of course. E-mail, instant messaging, blogging, and cellphones are not technology to Millennials any more than telephones are technology to Boomers. Millennials are adept at cutting and pasting offerings to get what they want out of them, creating an entirely customized world for themselves in the process.

Perhaps a bit on the naive side in terms of information literacy and validating knowledge, Millennials as students are eager and willing to participate in team projects although they benefit from clear direction and perhaps a few more-seasoned individuals on the team. Of all the generations, the Millennials are the most comfortable and confident with change. They have high expectations of distance learning and, because of this, can be the hardest group to satisfy. Since this generation is only beginning to enter professional fields and joining the ranks of our instructor-colleagues, we may be somewhat in the dark about what Millennials think and feel about us or the learning experiences we offer.

Not incidentally, the characteristics of this up-and-coming market are well aligned with distance-learning approaches. In the next decade, the possibilities and opportunities for distance learning—whether for professional development, academic advancement, or personal study—will no doubt explode as Millennials become a larger part of the potential market and bring their tech orientation into the institutions they join and shape. Congratulations to them—they're on the leading edge of the trend!

The Endgame: Motivation and Learner-Centered Experiences

Developing an understanding of learner types, learning styles, and generational differences is an interesting exercise, but what do you as an instructor need to do with that information? Remember that it's not about you; it's about *them*. The more you know about them, the more you can choose and use effective distance-learning models, write student-focused content, develop activities that deepen (and test) learning, and craft the learning experience to meet students where they are.

Most of all, you now have the information you need to motivate your students. I can't say enough about the importance of motivation in creating successful learning experiences. All behavior, including the learning process, is motivated.

In traditional classroom environments, explicit attention to motivation is rarely part of the instructional equation. The student is assumed to be motivated by the sheer fact of his or her presence. In a distance-learning environment, an instructor who ignores the motivation of the students and the ways to enhance and deepen that motivation experiences attrition, missing-in-action students, and zero enrollments. Perhaps the key difference is that the environment *is* distance. Learning takes energy, and without constantly pushing on the motivation button (which gets pushed, however discreetly, whenever a student walks into a traditional classroom), it's easy for students to get discouraged or distracted.

Motivation is the secret ingredient in successful educational programs: no motivation, no learning.

In my own experience as a self-directed human being, the best motivation comes from the inside. Sure, I can do just about anything—for a little while—if I'm compelled from the outside to do it. I can do a one-day training just because I *have* to. But commit to the challenge and energy drain of a more in-depth learning experience? That takes positive, internal motivation to keep me going.

There's also a correlation between the amount of motivation a person needs to complete a task and the perceived difficulty of the task. Distance learning is perceived by many adults as difficult because it is unfamiliar. To overcome the perceived difficulty, students must have strong positive motivation.

Of course, motivation is a highly personal thing; what motivates one student will leave another completely cold. In interacting with individual students, a wise distance-learning instructor will work to discover an individual student's personal motivations and then work to enhance them by means of the content of the course and the feedback, thereby creating a meaningful, positive experience. (Chapter 6, which discusses instructor-student interactions, will provide specific tips on identifying motivators and maintaining motivation.)

Motivation can also be bolstered through the social nature of good distance-learning programs. Interaction with peers does more than provide fodder for team projects and gripe sessions about the crazy, unreasonable instructor. Buddying up supports commitment, whether for an exercise regimen or a learning regimen. Creating formal or informal mentorship programs between more- and less-experienced students or between students with complementary skills and interests can add to a dynamic in which the students are helping each other succeed.

The literature on successful computer-mediated education indicates that the presence of a virtual student lounge, where students can talk about anything and everything, contributes to the success of the overall learning environment. Even a place to share news and blow off a bit of steam can help students feel connected to each other and create the potential for a bit of peer-to-peer coaching when motivation is running low. (Chapter 7, which focuses on creating a community of learners, will identify ways an instructor can use group interactions to support individual motivation.)

Technology that dies at a critical moment, insensitive (or nonexistent) student support services, confusing assignments, late feedback, breaches of Netiquette (online etiquette) can erode a student's motivation. Instructors may have little control over some of these factors; the best they can do is try to anticipate trouble and respond quickly and appropriately when problems arise.

Adult Learners Need ...

Put together all this information about attitudes toward education, learning styles, and generational differences, and the picture that emerges is both simple and complex. It's simple in that you can now understand your students first as human beings and relate to them compassionately in a way that allows their differences to enhance the learning environment.

It's complex in that humans and their interactions are inherently complex; we can't connect intimately and effectively with everyone.

I don't mind admitting that I'm somewhat starry eyed about teaching. From my perspective, the instructor-student relationship calls on me to be my best and to encourage students to be their best. If I can create a safe environment for experimentation, a place where students recognize that they can learn from failure as well as success, an environment that makes me in some ways as vulnerable as the students themselves, then we all have a real opportunity to reimagine the possibilities of our abilities and potential.

Instructors can create this kind of rich, creative, and rigorous environment by providing adult learners with the following:

- **A Little TLC:** "Warm and encouraging" is always a good attitude to project. Care about your students as individuals, and communicate that caring. You don't need to fawn over them; just let them know you are a real human being who appreciates their own humanness.
- **Cheerleading and Coaching:** Celebrate success and find the teachable elements of failure. Make it clear that you're there to help, not out to get them. Know, too, that in a distance-learning environment, you may need to do some cheerleading and coaching to help students navigate the course itself, as well as mastering the skills it covers.
- **Collaborative Projects:** Teamwork pushes learning to a new level; in addition to mastering subject matter, students must work with the material in a group setting. Together, they discover more about what they know and what they need to learn. In distance learning in particular, collaborative work helps cement the relationships that create a community of learners.
- **Flexibility:** Keep an open mind when learning about your students' needs for different learning methods, time frames, or approaches to the material. In addition to the variations required by learning styles and busy schedules, you will likely learn something entirely new about a great way to teach.
- **Practical Usage:** Let's cut to the chase, as they say: Demonstrate the practical value of the knowledge students are gaining and

Not Working with Adults?

Even teenagers can benefit from this kind of approach to understanding the needs of learners. Although lacking in life experiences that are of critical value to adult learners, teens can thrive in an educational environment that helps them take charge of their learning, become more self-aware and self-confident, and create a customized path toward the learning objectives.

While you have their attention, it's a good idea, too, to plant the idea in their heads that their learning preferences may change over time. Today's teens will need to be life-long learners in order to make their way through life. Each instructor they encounter on the way has an opportunity to help them understand themselves as learners and the way their particular approach to learning can be an asset. Lay the foundation for formal and informal educational experiences by doing more than creating content-specific competence; teach the students, not the subject, and teach them something about themselves along the way.

allow them to apply the knowledge in the context of their own interests and experiences.

Now Let's Build a Course

Who knew there was so much to learn about the students before we can even start planning what to teach? No wonder so many educational programs focus on content—it's much easier to understand than students!

By now, you should have an idea of the kinds of students you may be working with, as well as the potential tools and technologies at your disposal. Complete Worksheet 2.1 on the following page to capture your ideas and knowledge about your student population. (A Web-based version of this worksheet and other tools can be found at www.electric-muse.com/tbyr.asp.) Now you are ready to tackle the actual creation of a course that will be appropriately designed for the needs of your students and the capabilities of your chosen technologies.

Worksheet 2.1 Understanding Students

Use this worksheet to understand your student population and what their educational needs may be.

Which generations are represented among your students?

Generations	**None**	**A Few**	**Many**	**Don't Know**
Matures				
Baby Boomers				
Generation X				
Millennials				

What are the most common motivators bringing your students into the classroom?

Please rate your agreement with the following statements, where 1 = completely disagree and 5 = completely agree:

My students...	**1**	**2**	**3**	**4**	**5**
Know they need what I am offering.					
Have clear goals in mind for pursuing education.					
Prefer environments in which they have a lot of choice and control.					
Prefer environments in which the path to success is very clear.					
Have access to technology.					
Live within driving distance of each other and of me.					
Are comfortable with technology.					
Take my class because they want to rather than because they have to.					
Are self-aware learners—they understand the circumstances that help them learn best.					
Have intense demands on their time, professionally and personally.					
Are under external pressure to succeed in my class.					
Believe in the value of classroom studies.					
Have taken distance classes before.					
Are confident in their abilities to learn.					

Other observations or insights about your students, based on your experience with them or with similar groups:

Use the information on this worksheet when you consider audiences in the instructional design process. Visit www.electric-muse.com/tbyr.asp for a Web-based version of this worksheet and other planning tools.

Chapter 3

Content, Part I: Instructional Design

Instructional design is an even more misunderstood profession than teaching. Just as subject expertise does not guarantee teaching skill, teaching expertise does not guarantee the ability to design and create effective learning experiences tuned to desired outcomes of teacher, organization, and student. Turning information delivery into instruction is the purview of instructional design.

What Is Instructional Design?

Instructional design is a process by which learning experiences are engineered on the basis of student needs, desired outcomes, and available tools and resources. Instructional designers need to

- Understand the student population
- Be familiar with the media of delivery and interaction
- Sift through and organize content
- Select appropriate methods for creating the optimum learning experience
- Establish the environment for learning
- Assess results and outcomes

No, it's not enough to be an expert in your subject matter, proficient in choosing tools and technologies, or able to conduct ad hoc student psychological analysis; now you also have to be an instructional designer. (No one ever said the glory of being a teacher would come easily.) Before writing and developing actual teaching materials, exercises, assignments, and activities (which we'll tackle in Chapter 4), you must create an instructional framework for your course.

Think of the instructional-design process as a kind of cartography. When you finish, you will have created a map indicating the various routes through the material, the stops along the way for activity and interaction, and the destination you and the students will reach when successful. The instructional-design process is invaluable for clarifying your thinking about what you want to share with students and coming up with creative ways to work with them across media and learning styles. The design process also serves as your guide to the actual content you need to create. After a few courses, you'll be able to eyeball your map and estimate how much time you will need to develop content for a new program.

The process and the resulting map have enormous collaborative value as well. Work through the design process with your distance-learning team, and you create shared understanding of the goals and requirements of the project. Or work through the process on your own and use the resulting map to brainstorm with your team to find the resources, approaches, tools, and technologies that will serve your course best.

Don't discount the possibility of adding a trained instructional designer to your team should you have access and budget. You can apply the principles of instructional design as laid out in this chapter on your own, but a trained designer draws upon education and experience as well as a professional focus on understanding instruction from the learner's perspective. If you don't have time or budget for a designer as a working part of your team, it might be worthwhile to hire one as a consultant for a few hours, just to get you started on the right path or review your design before implementation.

Most of the principles of instructional design apply equally to traditional and distance-learning environments. This chapter will first introduce the general principles and then examine some of the unique instructional design challenges of distance-learning programs. Finally, the worksheets and process description at the end of the chapter will guide you through the draft of a design for your course, either on your own or in collaboration with the rest of your development team.

Getting the Most Benefit from an Instructional Designer

If you are working with an instructional designer, don't skip this chapter! It will help you understand what the designer is up to, and it will put you on track to work in tandem with your designer to reach your goals.

Keep in mind that a designer does much more than translate your expertise into a syllabus and a test. Designers craft the learning experience so that students can do what they're supposed to be able to do when they complete the program. A creative, collaborative relationship between you and your designer requires that you learn something about the unique value this professional brings to the table.

One caveat, though: Many professionals have become de facto instructional designers without real background or training in the field. For instance, some software developers have been pushed into the role of instructional designer because they are the ones building an e-learning interface. Be sure your instructional designer is actually designing instruction and not a Web site!

General Instructional Design Principles

Start with the End in Mind

You can't get where you want to go unless you know where that is. So you must start with the end in mind: What can successful students say, think, or do once they have completed the course?

Notice how starting from the end and framing the question this way immediately shifts your thinking from *what to teach* to *why the student needs to learn*. That's a crucial shift and one that many instructors are unaccustomed to making. Furthermore, this shift prepares you to start thinking in terms of learner motivation; they *need* to learn, but do they *want* to learn?

Different Settings, Different Goals—Same Process

When I teach college communications courses through the University of Phoenix Online, I have very clear outcomes in mind. By the time students leave my class, they need to be able to research and write a passable paper for other courses in their programs of study. Along the way, I want them to start feeling good about the writing process and their own abilities. But the bottom line is how they perform: Can they write like a college student or not?

On the other hand, my students in Creative Writing in English at the University of Gävle in Sweden have much more individual and amorphous successful outcomes. Every semester, I work with a dozen or so students who have their own genre focus, level of expertise, and distinct personal goals for their creative writing. For a few, English is their native language, but this isn't the case for most who want to work on their language skills. It's a challenge to treat this class as a class and not as a series of mentored relationships. But if the participants are to benefit from being a group of learning peers, I need to have an instructional focus rather than simply respond to each student individually. Over time, I've developed an overarching instructional goal for my work with the class. No matter what kind of writing the students are doing or how they are developing as creative writers, my instructional goal is that they read literature and respond to it as creative writers rather than simply as readers. If I were to write down a learning objective for this course, it might be this: Students will identify specific writing techniques found in literature of their choosing and apply those techniques in their own creative work. In other words, I'm pushing them to see themselves and their work within the broader context of world literature.

These are two very different kinds of classes with very different kinds of goals. Yet in both cases, the presence of these goals provides me with a framework in which to focus my instruction. We're not floundering for something to do, and I'm not simply reacting to what a student turns in. There's too much to know about writing to teach the class without specific goals. The same is true for any area of instruction.

Learning Objectives

Instructional goals often translate directly into learning objectives. Learning objectives are succinct, learner-focused statements of defined, measurable outcomes for the course. In the planning and development process, learning objectives create checks and balances for me to use in reviewing a draft outline or an assignment for a course: Does this project satisfy the learning objective? Does this assignment give learners enough information and practice to subsequently achieve an objective?

Learning objectives need to be targeted, specific, and measurable. Here are some examples of learning objectives written to meet these criteria:

- Students will correctly identify and format the parts of a business letter.
- Participants will accurately apply the three steps of analysis to solve the problem presented in the case study.
- Trainees will operate a forklift under normal warehouse conditions while achieving a safety score of at least 99 percent.

Notice how these objectives are

- Action oriented
- Measurable
- Learner focused
- Grounded in a specific condition or context for action

Learning to write objectives is similar to learning to write haiku. "Condensed and specific" describes both art forms. The impact is also similar—both create a universe shared between reader and writer with the fewest words possible.

Keep in mind that you may have implicit or hidden objectives as well as explicit objectives. For instance, whenever I teach a course comprised of many students who are new to distance learning, one of my objectives is that they successfully complete the assigned activities in all areas of the course. Whether I ever express that objective to students depends on the groups and our relationship, but knowing that it *is* an objective ensures that I monitor progress toward that particular goal.

Despite my appreciation for learning objectives, I feel that they are overused in course materials. Current standard practices suggest that learning objectives should be placed prominently at the beginning of

Words to Use in Learning Objectives

Verbs that result in an observable action are best to use:

- list
- identify
- state
- describe
- define
- solve
- compare and contrast
- operate

Avoid verbs that result in actions that are difficult or impossible to quantify:

- know
- use
- understand
- see

distance-learning materials so students are prepared for what they are about to learn. That practice can create problems. Read the following learning objective (adapted from the excellent library of articles and resources provided by Kevin Kruse at his site, e-LearningGuru, www.e-learningguru.com), and try not to roll your eyes:

After completing this course, you will be able to

- Place a caller on hold
- Activate the speaker phone
- Play new messages on the voice mail system
- List the three elements of a proper phone greeting
- Transfer a call to a requested extension

I know these are important skills (I've accidentally hung up on more than one caller when I was learning a new phone system), but from a student's perspective, it's impossible to take them seriously as learning objectives. Just reading them, I feel particularly disinclined to participate in the training and mildly insulted.

Learning objectives are raw material, not final content. Use them for planning, focus, and development purposes, but be sure you translate them into learner-friendly objectives before you launch your course. Go back to motivation: Make objectives clear, but also make them compelling and learner focused. In Chapter 4, we'll look specifically at ways to communicate learning objectives without alienating, insulting, or boring your students.

How Many Objectives?

The number of learning objectives you need for any course depends on a host of factors. Clearly, a self-contained training module needs far fewer objectives than a semester-long college seminar. How much you break down large objectives into smaller pieces will also have an impact on the final number. Programs can be built on as few as one objective. Most of my college courses have between six and eight; professional education, development, and training, which I usually teach in 5-week sessions, generally involve four to six objectives. If I find that I have substantially more than that on my working list, it's an indication that I'm trying to cram too much into a course.

Scope of Content

One of the hardest parts of developing content for a course is editing. You have sophisticated knowledge of a subject, and you are eager to share that knowledge with learners who need and want it. It's hard to say no to anything that could add to the learner's appreciation for the topic. Yet learners are not ready for everything a topic expert knows; throwing too much at them (unless they are highly motivated and have powerful incentives to persist) will overwhelm them. The result? Attrition, poor motivation, confusion, dissatisfaction, and zero outcomes (and then where's your funding going to come from?).

Selecting which areas of content to cover requires a topic expert to step back into the learner's shoes. Return to the overall goals: What should a learner be able to say, think, or do after completing a course? More importantly, what does a learner want to be able to say, think, or do? Where's the pain that the learner is turning to education to assuage? The best content to choose is the material that will directly address that pain.

Throughout the learning experience, of course, a skilled instructor also plants the seeds for deepened engagement with the topic: "You got great results from *this*! But just wait till you see what you can do once you've learned *that*!" Aha! Now the learner is internally motivated to bite off a bigger chunk.

It's tempting to put it all in, but you risk losing your students entirely by giving them too much irrelevant instruction. Sure, you may know that it is incredibly relevant, but the learner remains dissatisfied. Overstuffed courses or courses that are too far from the pain do not encourage deep interaction of learners with the materials, the instructor, or the other students. Students have little chance to find meaning for themselves in the information, and so it remains in the "training" file, never to be put into action.

Or look at it as self-preservation: If you insist on covering *everything*, you will end up with a course that takes much longer than it should to prepare and deliver. Remember that adult learners are battered with competing demands for their time; you're probably feeling a bit of that yourself. Be realistic or you are setting yourself and your students up for frustration. If, on the other hand, their learning experience is exciting and produces the results they want, they will be motivated to take the next step and commit more deeply with you and the material.

Have I convinced you yet? If you just can't help yourself, here are some tips to save your sanity:

- Create "deeper reading" and optional assignments that delve into critical areas that you don't have room for in the syllabus. Make these materials available after the end of the course, perhaps as a self-paced add-on, to support those who are motivated to continue.
- Review your entire course against your learning objectives; is anything a bit off-topic? Consider making it optional or moving it to a different course altogether.

- Review the number and complexity of learning objectives; can you focus on a smaller number of objectives in this one offering? Can you simplify any of the objectives to reduce the amount of content you need to cover?
- Allow potential students to preview your course, including objectives, topics, and materials, and give their impressions of the appropriateness, complexity, time commitment, and focus of the course. Listen to their feedback!
- Ask an instructional designer, if you have one on your team or can corner one, to run a professional eye over what you are creating. Instructional designers have professional skill in matching content to expectations.
- Offer courses in a series, or develop an outline for additional courses you could offer if there is sufficient interest. Don't pour hours of your time into courses that your audiences aren't ready for yet—and possibly don't even know they need.

Eventually, you have to make your choices and live with them. Select the topics you will cover, based on your goals and objectives, the needs of the students, and the smallest portion of material you feel is necessary for the students to reach the objectives within the time frame of the program.

Events of Instruction

When I taught entirely in traditional classrooms or in one-on-one mentoring situations, I never gave a thought to the mental processes required for a student to learn what I was teaching. Once I moved into a distance environment, however, the necessity of planning *everything* in advance pushed me to learn more about creating readiness on the part of my learners and then maximizing that readiness by delivering effective instruction.

Robert Gagne is known in behaviorist circles as the father of instructional design and training. (Did you even know there were behaviorist circles? There's a specialty for everything.) In his 1965 book, *The Conditions of Learning*, Gagne first identified and described the mental conditions for adult learning:

- Capture attention: Directing and focusing the students' attention activates their "learning receptors."
- Inform learners of objectives: Students need to know what to expect of the learning experience; informing them of objectives sets their expectations and prepares them properly for entry into the learning experience.
- Stimulate recall of prior learning: By building on existing knowledge, whether tacit or explicit, students can prepare to encode new information in their short-term memories.
- Present the content: The instructor makes a selective presentation of material, filtering it for students so they understand its context and meaning.
- Provide "learning guidance": By interacting with the material under the guidance of an instructor, students begin to understand its meaning and relevance to their needs. This step begins the process of encoding the information in long-term memory.
- Elicit performance (practice): Students practice or work directly with skills and concepts to demonstrate understanding, deepen the encoding process, and verify the accuracy of their understanding.
- Provide feedback: Instructors and peers reinforce performance by providing assessment and correction.
- Enhance retention and transfer: Students begin to generalize their newly acquired knowledge and apply it in other situations.

Too often, instructors jump into presenting the content without attending to the earlier events. As a result, students must scramble to catch up—or drop the course. At the instructional design stage, make sure your design covers the entire continuum of instructional events: You have to capture their attention and carry them through to generalization of their new knowledge. In Chapter 4, we'll be spending more time with the events of instruction and their impact on writing and creating actual instructional materials.

Activity-Based Learning

Presentational instruction—for example, standing at a podium and delivering a lecture, jazzed up, perhaps, with a visual presentation—is hardly an optimal model for education of any kind. Yet "talk and test" is a common model—one you may even be unconsciously following. Adult learners need practical, results-oriented learning experiences. Activity-based learning can meet those needs while moving them along the continuum of instructional events.

As you review your topics and objectives, ask yourself one question over and over: "How could this be an activity?" Here are some answers you might come up with:

- Conduct an interview
- Role-play with classmates or other colleagues
- Conduct an experiment
- Participate in a survey and compare responses to an aggregated benchmark
- Respond to reflective questions in a private journal
- Respond to content questions in a public discussion
- Complete a simulation
- Fix a software bug

Don't worry yet about creating assignments or even figuring out how you can get students to do the activity within the context of a distance-learning environment. Focus on generating a long and interesting list of relevant, engaging activities that will help students move along the path to achieving their (and your) objectives.

Evaluation and Assessment

How will you know whether your course is effective? The best test of effectiveness is the performance of the learners when they take their learning back to the real world. Unless they have the ability to assess performance following a course, most instructors resort to testing of some kind.

When students are earning credit for completing a course, at either a college or their workplace, evaluation becomes even more important. In such cases, it's extremely helpful to have evaluation tools that can help you review the work of individual students against a single standard of excellence. When grading essays for my University of Phoenix Online communications students, I always use a rubric in which I score the paper in particular areas (see Figure 3.1); otherwise, grading a writing assignment can become far too subjective. For the students' sake, and for my own, I need to work from an established standard.

Consider, too, what *you* consider to be a successful outcome for your course. If, for instance, you regularly lose one-third to one-half of your students by the midpoint in the program, something is not working. That's a kind of assessment-in-action.

Distance-Learning Design Particulars

Most elements of instructional design are common to both traditional and distance-learning environments. Some elements have unique considerations in distance learning, however, and these are described in the rest of this chapter.

Nonlinear Information

In a traditional classroom, an instructor presents ideas sequentially because the classroom is governed by the clock. An instructor moves in a linear fashion from one idea to the next throughout the classroom period as well as the term of the course.

In a distance-learning program, you still have the option of moving sequentially, but you are no longer bound by that model. You can present materials simultaneously, in concert with one another, in parallel or intersecting tracks, or just about any other way you can imagine. And your students will probably find even more ways to move through the materials.

One example of a way to break off from the sequential pathway can be found in some computer games my 6-year-old daughter likes to play. These games involve various problem-solving activities built around a narrative that takes the main characters through the environments within the game.

My daughter can choose to follow the narrative, or she can jump to the particular activities she feels like doing at the moment.

Similarly, a distance-learning experience could be designed to enable a student to access any activity or area at any time rather than moving along the standard "narrative," the chronological progression primarily intended by the instructor. Such a design could be challenging to combine with peer-to-peer interaction, but an instructor could work around that challenge by requiring students to navigate the course with one or two other students in small learning groups.

Checklist for Effective Writing (1 [low]–5 [high])

What is the point? (Content) ____ of 12 possible points

____ Student accomplished the objectives of the assignment.
____ Student clearly demonstrates understanding of the subject matter at appropriate depth.
____ Ideas and information presented are adequate; data is not limited or missing.
____ Paper is clear, focused, and interesting.
____ Paper includes relevant material and conveys more than a general message.
____ Adequate support is provided for assertions.
____ The ability to link theory to practical experience is evident.

How well was the point made? (Organization) ____ of 8 possible points

____ Organization emphasizes the central theme or purpose.
____ Paper demonstrates a determination of audience and is appropriate to that audience.
____ Each paragraph contains only one main idea, logically developed.
____ Information is properly sequenced throughout the paper.

Is the paper professionally presented? (Format) ____ of 5 possible points

____ Paper has been carefully edited.
____ Paper is professional in appearance.
____ Paper conforms to MLA/APA standards for format and citation of sources.

Was the writing effective? (Readability) ____ of 5 possible points

____ Student used short words and sentences appropriately.
____ Word choices convey the message in an interesting, precise, and natural way.
____ Student selected an appropriate writing strategy and style.
____ Sentences are well built, with strong but varied structure.
____ Sentences are fluid.
____ Student used powerful verbs, active voice, and appropriate vocabulary.
____ Paper is not excessively wordy or full of redundancies.

Was the writing grammatically correct? (Grammar, Punctuation) ____ of 5 possible points

____ No shifts in tense or voice are evident.
____ Student avoids colloquial expressions and jargon.
____ Pronoun referents are clear.
____ Proper grammar and punctuation are used.

Total points: ____ of 35 possible points

Figure 3.1 A copy of the rubric I use for grading written papers. The rubric keeps me focused on learning objectives and specific areas for improvement.

Another example of a nonlinear approach is Web site design. The familiarity many adults have with navigating nonlinear Web sites enables them to work with instructional materials built on the same model. Although the instructor will have to find ways to boost the peer power of such a learning environment, it can be an effective approach, particularly in courses implemented on a Web-based platform and for students who are more highly motivated in situations in which they have greater control.

Customization

Presentational instruction, such as that found in lecture halls, allows for little or no customization on the part of the learner. The instructor presents the material; the student takes notes and may have an opportunity to ask questions. Any customization happens outside the main educational environment. Instructors may teach to the least able students, expecting that others will tune in and out as their attention is piqued, or instructors may teach to those students in the middle, hoping that the less able ones will struggle to catch up or drop the course. Or instructors may just present whatever they want to present, without giving much thought to the abilities of the students in the lecture hall.

Move into a distance-learning environment and customization becomes a more natural part of how students encounter the content, the instructor, and their peers, thus building their own learning based on their preferences and abilities. Students may access a page in a Web-based course where they can opt to play a video, download and read an article or transcript, or view the original research that went into the video, annotated by the instructor. Students may receive an instructor's mailed feedback as handwritten notes or as an audio recording of comments. Students may call in for a teleconference, call up the archived tape of the conference at a later date, access and search the audio file online, or even download a transcript of the entire call.

It's easy in distance learning to forget about providing options, perhaps because just getting the course pulled together and created is challenge enough. But students who are able to choose their learning methods, choose among activities, and access the material in a way that best suits their style are the students who excel and leave satisfied.

Choosing Your Tools

Your choice of tools for distance learning has, of course, an enormous impact on your students, your development process, your budget, and the kinds of skills your team needs. If you are using Web-enabled interactions for any part of your course, you need to work closely with the developers who design, build, test, and support the tools you use for interaction. If you are using print materials (such as workbooks) for your course, you need to find graphic designers with skill in instructional materials. Even if you are relying on e-mail and telephone systems for delivering distance learning, you need partners or vendors who can support those functions and advise you on your choices.

Many instructors don't have much of a choice of the tools they can use; their sponsoring organizations have contracted with Web-based course management providers, and they are required to use those tools to develop and deliver their courses. However, those systems come with just about every imaginable feature, allowing you to choose which tools you want in your distance-learning environment. You still get to decide if you want to use the whiteboard, the chat room, the private journal, the learning groups, the glossary, or any of the other amazing functions that are literally at your fingertips.

Sometimes when you are working collaboratively with distance-learning development teams, it may feel like you're speaking different languages. In fact, you probably are. Software folks think the way software thinks, which may not be your particular cup of tea.

The best way to bring out the best in everyone's skill set is to focus the discussion on outcomes rather than functions. Tell your designer, developer, or overall tech guru the outcome you want to create. For example:

Not: Let's include a synchronous chat section.

But: I'd like students to have a secure space in which they can have real-time discussion with access to the course readings.

Not: I saw this cool multimedia thing in a friend's classroom; let's do that.

But: I have video that I want to be able to play, stop and start, and search. Students will need to be able to access the video both

> during the real-time session and on their own. Oh, and I want some of the sections of the video to be linked to key sections in the glossary and reserve readings. What do you think we should use?

Be willing to try something new and experimental, but also be firm in pushing your partners to find the simplest solution to your challenge. Does it need a technology-intense solution, or can something low tech do the job? By moving to the lowest possible technology, you give yourself more room to maneuver. Costs and development times decrease, which means it will be easier to make changes or updates. Furthermore, from the students' perspective, using the lowest possible technology makes the materials more accessible, physically and psychologically.

Putting the "Process" in the Design Process

By now, it's probably clear that planning and designing a distance-learning course requires your brain to multitask. There are so many factors to take into consideration, and the enterprise is further complicated because many different individuals need to be part of the development process.

Worksheet 3.1 provides a format for group or individual brainstorming. Use or adapt it to ensure you are covering all the critical steps in crafting the design of your distance-learning offering. If you are working in a group, use the worksheet to guide your discussion, moving from one section to the next. If you are working on your own, simply follow the organizational structure of the worksheet.

At the end of the brainstorming session, you should have a solid edited list of primary content areas for your course, as well as a long list of possible activities in each area. It's a good idea to come up with more ideas than you can possibly use; go for outlandish as well as tried and true. Let your collaborative partners provide technical input into activities—your software developer may have a great idea for a virtual simulation, while your graphic designer may have a brilliant flash of insight regarding a workbook component.

Figure 3.2 shows what Worksheet 3.1 might look like when completed; Figure 3.3 translates the information graphically into a mind map. You'll see how this is already starting to look like a workplan for building a

Worksheet 3.1 Instructional Design and Planning

Course name (tentative):

Description:

Who are the students? (Refer to the Worksheet 2.1)

Where is their pain? What do they most want to get out of the course?

Course goals:

Draft learning objectives:

What are the challenges?

Topic areas:

Activities:

Verbs to use in learning objectives:
- list
- identify
- state
- describe
- define
- solve
- compare and contrast
- operate

course, as well as a content outline you can follow to create your instructional content.

You will not hit on the perfect design the first time you try, any more than Henry Ford made it big with Models A, B, or C. But getting it on paper, talking through the problems and opportunities with others, and working through a process will enable you to design a course that is both exciting and educational for you and your students.

Crafting a Topic Syllabus

The last step of the design stage is to craft a topic syllabus for your course. (Did you wonder if we'd ever get here?) The syllabus should capture all the main areas of the course and lay out the primary pathway through the topics, materials, and activities (see Figure 3.4).

Syllabi for distance-learning courses are more complex than the ones you may have used for traditional courses. When I write syllabi for traditional courses, I usually include basic information like required reading, course description, my contact information, a run-down of topics, and the time frames for completing assignments. I treat my syllabi for distance-learning courses as a contract between the students and me. Everything from participation requirements to grading for specific assignments to an overview of Netiquette expectations goes into the syllabus. All that information makes for a long syllabus, and I also repeat much of the critical information in stand-alone documents that students can access when needed. But the time and energy I put into creating detailed, comprehensive syllabi are more than offset by the value of having a single, controlling document to establish the parameters of the course.

For now, though, your draft topic syllabus serves primarily as your content development guide. It will surely change between now and the launch of your course, but at this stage of the process, it tells you and your development team what to write, design, build, and create to construct a distance-learning environment.

Course name (tentative):

The "M" Word: What Rabbis need to know about marketing
Synagogue Marketing
Marketing as a Mitzvah

Description:
A five-week online workshop on the basics of synagogue marketing—what it is, how to do it, and what resources you already have so that you don't have to spend a fortune to get results!

Who are the students? (Refer to Worksheet 2.1):
Rabbis (?)
Synagogue staff
Volunteers
May have some marketing background; for most this will be the first online course ever

Where is their pain? What do they most want to get out of the course?
They know they need to be doing something different, but they don't know what. Most think of marketing as equal to advertising—need to start to see it as about relationships and about current members as well as prospective members.

They need practical tools so that the process isn't too "heady" or time-consuming. If it's too difficult, expensive, or labor-intensive, they will keep doing what they're doing.

Course goals:
Introduce concepts of strategic marketing
Reorient synagogue to audiences
Learn to tap existing resources
Write and maintain a marketing plan that is practical and measurable

Draft learning objectives:
- List the three goals of marketing
- Identify and characterize internal and external audiences
- Apply the course templates to write draft press releases, flyers and notices
- Create a practical marketing plan with defined measures of success
- Identify existing resources for low-cost and no-cost marketing
- Compare and contrast print, electronic and word-of-mouth marketing methods

Verbs to use in learning objectives:
- list
- identify
- state
- describe
- define
- solve
- compare and contrast
- operate

Figure 3.2 Sample of Worksheet 3.1 completed. This shows what the instructional design team came up with in our initial meetings for Marketing as a Mitzvah, an online workshop to train rabbis, synagogue staff, and volunteers in synagogue marketing.

What are the challenges?

Use of a technology-based platform will be challenging for some participants
Time—everyone is overworked
Concept may be unsettling to many at first—think of synagogues as antithetical to "marketing"

Topic areas:

Definitions of marketing
Understanding Audiences
Public relations
Research and measurement
Copyright
Design
Web and e-communications
Low-cost and no-cost methods
Finding, training and managing volunteers for marketing

Activities:

- Evaluate current marketing tools
- Write a wish list for marketing tools
- Write a volunteer job description
- Research a public relations list
- Craft and implement a survey
- Compare and contrast marketing materials from different organizations
- Conduct a focus group and report back
- Run a brainstorming session on updating and improving the print newsletter
- Journal entries comparing expectations to new knowledge

Figure 3.2 (*cont.*)

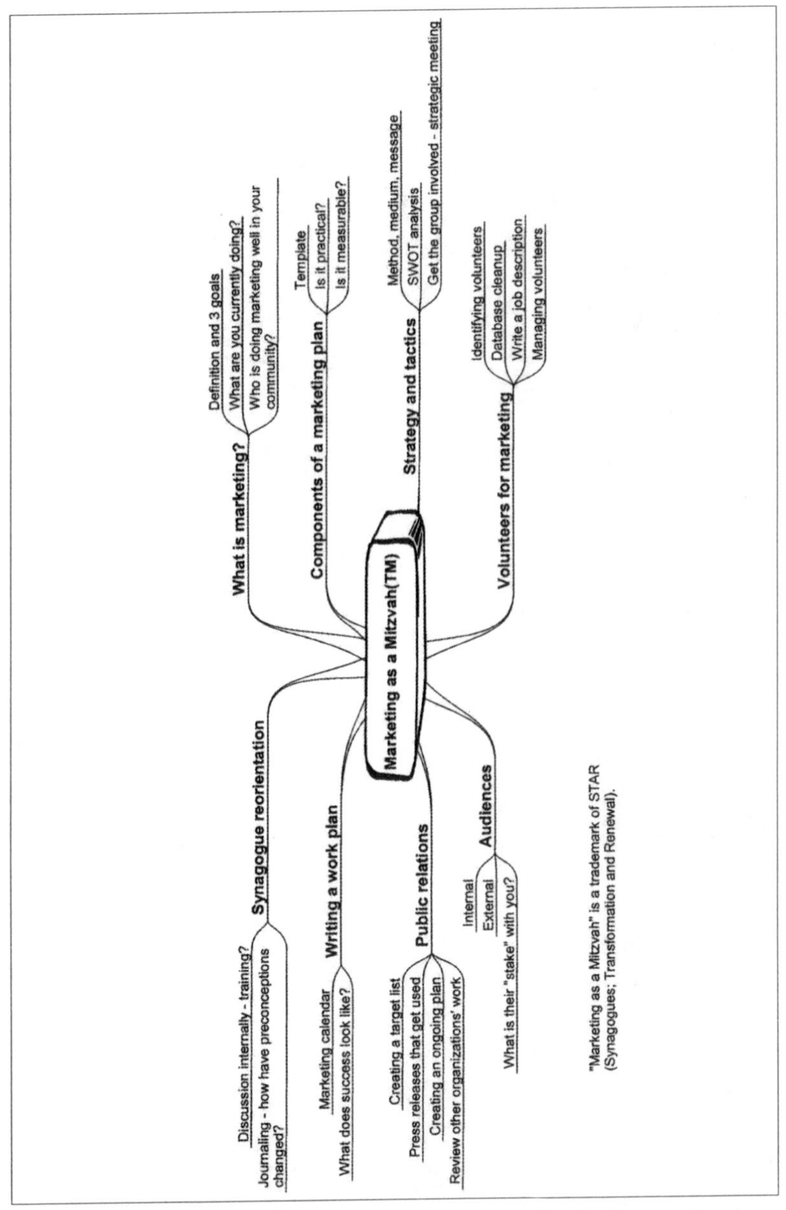

Figure 3.3 Marketing as a Mitzvah mind map. Draft mind map, showing the key topics for Marketing as a Mitzvah, as well as potential activities in each of the areas. The mind map also captures insights from our brainstorming session on the needs and characteristics of the audience and other considerations for the course.

Main topics, with activity ideas for each topic:

1. What is marketing?
   a. List current tool and code for which goal each works towards
   b. Get member feedback via a survey on use of each kind of tool
   c. Gather and analyze marketing materials from other organizations
2. Components of a marketing plan
   a. Fill in a template
   b. Critique a draft plan—what looks like it will work? How can you craft a hypothesis around it?
3. Strategy and tactics
   a. Method, medium, message worksheet
   b. SWOT analysis
   c. Strategic planning session, with discussion guide—conduct the session and report back to the class
4. Identifying volunteers
   a. Database review and cleanup
   b. Networking—you know someone who knows someone
   c. Write a job description
5. Identifying audiences
   a. Review SWOT analysis
   b. Audience "tree"
   c. Member database analysis
6. Public relations
   a. Research media contacts
   b. Use template to write a press release
   c. Gather and analyze press releases from other organizations
7. Workplan and measurement
   a. Complete the marketing calendar
   b. "What is measurement?" worksheet
8. Re-orientation of synagogue
   a. Discussion guide—conduct internal meeting and report back
   b. Journal—how is this concept of marketing different from what you expected?

Figure 3.4 Draft topic syllabus for Marketing as a Mitzvah.

Chapter 4

Content, Part II: Development

You've survived all that planning; now get ready for the flurry of activity that is content development. (Cue triumphal music.)

Not all distance-learning programs require that the instructor participate in crafting content. Some programs provide detailed content with which an instructor must teach—lectures, assignments, even a template syllabus. For example, the University of Phoenix Online has implemented a system of course delivery in which I am provided with 70–90 percent of the materials I need. This system enables me to prep a new class in the minimum amount of time and simultaneously ensures that students are experiencing comparable learning environments despite differences in instructor styles and mode of delivery (traditional classroom, blended approaches, or all online).

Many content-management software providers also make available libraries of courses that instructors can access and offer "off the shelf" or with minimal customization. Courses are available on a range of topics across the academic and professional spectrum. Some libraries are organized around "reusable learning objects," which instructors can plug into their courses or mix and match to create their course du jour.

Even when working with supplied course materials, however, a distance-learning instructor should know what goes into crafting effective, targeted, and engaging content. In the first place, the existence and availability of content is no guarantee of quality; if you find something you like, you still need to be able to evaluate its quality for your purposes and be able to adapt, improve, or jettison anything that isn't up to your standards. In the second place, even courses that are terrific right out of the box require instructors to create a bridge between the material and the students—to be the human interface that enables learning experiences. When I teach University of Phoenix courses for the online campus, I am required to use the course materials exactly as I have been trained to, but I still have to write my own greetings, provide instructions about how I prefer to receive assignments, write feedback, add supplementary lectures if I perceive a need for more depth, and respond immediately and appropriately to student needs.

Although it is possible to be a distance-learning instructor and have only a minimal need to create materials, it's an extremely limiting position to put yourself in. If you have any desire to create unique courses, based on your personal skills, experience, and interests, you will eventually need to write and co-develop the majority of material with which students will interact.

Creating content is a daunting task, but it can also be an exhilarating challenge (not unlike writing a book). And the process is iterative: You'll write, teach, rewrite, and re-organize on the basis of what you learned the first time around. In that way, it's quite similar to what you may experience the first few times you teach any new course in a traditional format.

The critical difference, of course, is interface. Whether you are creating printed instructions or animated, hands-on simulations, distance instruction means that you have to anticipate student questions and needs before they occur and build both questions and answers into the content itself. In addition, you must be able to write appropriately for the chosen medium and learn the right balance of textual, visual, and other kinds of information. At the same time, you also have to keep in mind and work with the events of instruction discussed in Chapter 3: gain attention, declare objectives, stimulate recall of prior learning, present content, provide guidance, elicit performance, provide feedback, and enable transfer of skills. And don't forget the specific needs and quirks of your student population, whether those quirks are generational, skill based, or attitudinal.

You aren't creating the course content so much as the container for learning experiences, taking into consideration all the different elements that make up the experience. How do students encounter the material? How are their expectations raised? How are they prepared to learn? How are they invited to interact with you, the other students, and the material? How do they learn the criteria for success, and how are they motivated to perform? When I'm working on the material for a course, I'm telling a narrative in my head—how Susie and Sam Student join the class, review and interact with the material, and successfully perform to my rigorous standards.

It's much more complicated than writing a lecture, and it's utterly and completely different from writing an academic paper. Creating content for a distance-learning course is like assuming responsibility for building management (Is it too hot? Too cold? Locked when the students show up? Drinking fountain out of order?) in addition to prepping to teach.

Get It in Writing

Most of this chapter deals with written language for two reasons. First, I am a writer, so I tend to see most challenges as solvable through writing. (My graphic designer friends see most challenges as solvable through visual organization; we make a good team.) But more importantly, written language plays a central role in creating effective distance courses. Written materials (online or off) are the most common point of interaction for instructors and students in distance learning.

Among the materials you will be writing regularly are the following:

- Course descriptions
- Lectures and explanatory materials
- Assignments and instructions
- Feedback to students
- Classroom commentary (in online discussion environments)
- Policy and procedure documents
- Syllabi
- Casual messages to students and colleagues

In addition to your writing tasks, you may be skilled (or interested in developing skills) in some of the technical arts that support your job as instructor: Web design, graphic design, programming and animation, technical support services, and more. For the purposes of this book, however, I am assuming that you have a support team or other professionals handling those areas. We'll look at their impact on content development from the perspective of what you as the instructor need to know and how you can contribute to the process. Appendix A lists readings and resources that address the technical and administrative aspects of distance-course development.

Where to Begin?

The course map and draft syllabus you completed in Chapter 3 is the place to start outlining and identifying the specific tasks and elements that you need to create before you will be ready for students. Figures 3.3 and 3.4 show the mind map and draft topic syllabus for "Marketing as a Mitzvah," a five-module professional development course I developed for Synagogues: Transformation and Renewal (STAR) (www.star synagogue.org) for its work with synagogue professionals and volunteers. Figure 3.2 shows the results of the syllabus-crafting step of our design process, including ideas for activities and important considerations for a single topic within the course. The three documents shown in those figures guide me in deciding what material I need to develop.

A Quick Peek at the End Result

Before we look at the step-by-step process for developing content, however, let's take a quick look at the end result to see where we're going. (Good distance-learning principle: Work with the end in mind!) This brief tour of the construction of the course will clarify how you can use the principles of instructional design, particularly the events of instruction, to develop materials. Instructional events are set in **boldface** type throughout.

Figure 4.1 shows the welcome page for Marketing as a Mitzvah. The purpose of this page is to capture the students' **attention** and **inform** them of some of the expectations for the course. "Discussions" indicates that discussion will be part of their work, and "Resource Center" tells them that they will have access to resources. "Weekly Activities" tells them to check a page weekly.

Seem too obvious to be instructionally driven? Consider what might happen to a student who came upon a home page that said only "Marketing as a Mitzvah: Click Here to Enter." Who would be brave enough to enter into goodness-knows-what? Who would find it an interesting enough headline to capture their attention? The course welcome page provides enough information to stimulate the first two events of instruction while guiding the student into the content.

Figure 4.2 shows one page of lecture content for the same course. Now the events of instruction are embedded in the content itself. The graphic headline at the top of the lecture **captures attention**. The first paragraph

Figure 4.1 Marketing as a Mitzvah welcome page. *(Used with permission of STAR, www.starsynagogue.org, and JSkyway, www.jskway.com)*

is also written to **capture attention** as well as **inform** the students about the topic and objectives on this page of content. The content is placed in a universally understood context, which **stimulates prior (if unconscious) learning** about what it means to do marketing in a synagogue setting. Then the text **presents the specific content** I want to teach in this section of the course. Near the end of the lecture, I provide the students with specific actions for **"encoding" the new information** in their memory and behavior. Finally, the **assignment reiterates encoding** and **elicits performance**.

But it doesn't stop there. Following completion of the assignment, students are asked to respond in the Discussions section with comments about their results. As a group, we discuss the outcomes of their efforts, **providing feedback** as well as helping them **transfer and expand the new knowledge** to other areas of their work.

For each element of any course I develop, I consider carefully where it fits within the overall arc of the students' learning experiences and make sure that I know where they are within the events of instruction.

Marketing in a Synagogue Context

Over the past two years, and particular in the development and execution of the **Synaplex Initiative**, STAR and its advisors have put emphasis on the "M" word - marketing. Within the nonprofit world (synagogues being a specific form of nonprofit organization), marketing is not a concept that many professionals are comfortable with. Marketing sounds like crass commercialism - a shifty process by which companies sell more detergent rather than something a spiritual, communal and social organization should be involved with.

It's time for some re-education about what marketing truly is and how synagogues can and should use it to develop deeper relationships with members, unaffiliated individuals and families, and other organizations.

Figure 4.2 Marketing as a Mitzvah lecture content. *(Used with permission of STAR, www.starsynagogue.org, and JSkyway, www.jskway.com)*

Activities First

The path from course map to completed content is simple enough to navigate if you follow a process. (Note that "simple" is not the same as "easy"—this stuff stretches your brain in all sorts of new directions.) Because successful adult learning is predicated on learner-focused, practical, relevant *activities*, they are the first content element I create. Once the activities are put into place, I can back up and reflect on what information, knowledge, or conditions students need to complete the activity successfully.

Pull out those learning objectives. Is there a culminating activity that would enable students to demonstrate mastery of most or all of the course objectives? Such an activity usually makes an effective final project. Again, consider what is practical and relevant for your students; if they come out of your course with a piece of work they can immediately apply to soothe their pain, you've hit the jackpot.

Back to Those Learning Objectives

Remember the list of objectives that told us we were going to learn to use the telephone? What do you do with those kinds of objectives to make them effective within your course materials?

You have to inform learners of objectives so that they can be prepared. Clearly communicated objectives also correlate with satisfaction; if students know what they're getting into, they're more likely to be happy with the result.

But you cannot and must not present doofy objectives (like "place calls on hold") to adults and expect them to respect you in the morning! The key to incorporating learning objectives into your course materials is to craft them in a way that connects with the learner's emotional commitment to learning. Speak to the pain (ah, that useful pain):

"It's 9 A.M. on your first day at the job you've been dreaming of. You are set for your first meeting and have your notebook and pen all warmed up and ready to go. But the phone rings. The phone rings? No one has your number yet. You pick it up and state your name with confidence. Wrong number, of course, but the caller wants you to transfer her to *your boss's* boss."

"Not to worry; you've completed the telephone training module, and you can transfer calls! Not bad for your first hour on the job."

It's a lot lengthier than "You will be able to transfer calls and put callers on hold." But it's also more motivating and more emotionally engaging. Most importantly, it communicates the learning objective without boring the learner.

For Marketing as a Mitzvah, for example, the culminating activity is for the participants to write an actionable, practical, measurable marketing plan for their synagogue. Working backward from the culminating activity then, I need to consider what stepping-stone activities will help them complete the final project. Figure 4.3 lays out possible activities for each topic area to develop knowledge and skills leading up to the final project.

Notice that I've struck a number of good ideas from the list. For instance, the entire area of volunteer recruiting, while critical to a successful synagogue marketing plan, is too much for this course; I make a note to create some add-on materials the participants can use on their own following the course to help them develop better practices in volunteer recruiting. (In fact, STAR and I have developed a full course dedicated to volunteer engagement, in part due to demand from those who successfully completed Marketing as a Mitvah.)

Through a process of review, editing, comparison with the learning objectives, and head scratching, I come up with a final list of two or three activities for each topic area, leading up to the culminating project (see Figure 4.4). It's not perfect; there are always areas of study I wish we would have time to cover and activities I know they'd enjoy but that are not directly relevant. Still, when I look at the final list, I'm confident that this is the right balance of activities to enable the participants to succeed.

Since activities are where students "get busy," you want to design them to hit the appropriate events of instruction. Activities can help students encode new information, practice skills, and even get feedback, depending on how the activity is designed. One of the activities assigned early in

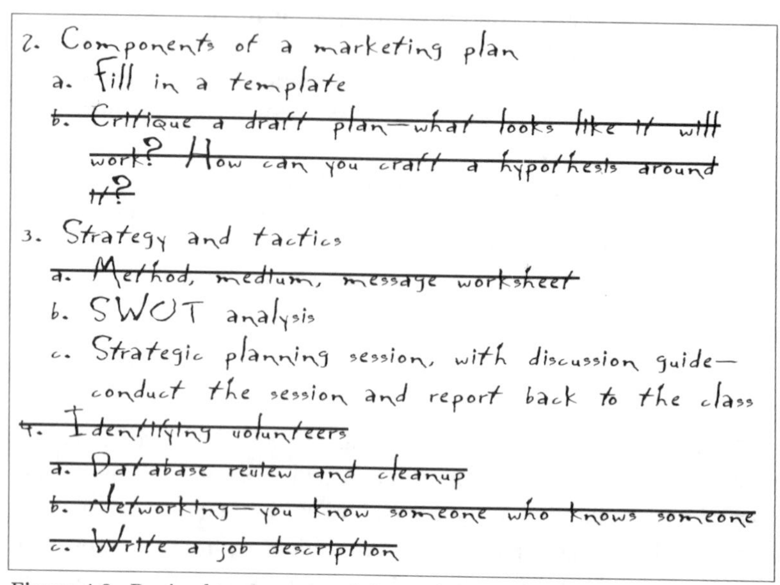

2. Components of a marketing plan
   a. Fill in a template
   ~~b. Critique a draft plan—what looks like it will work? How can you craft a hypothesis around it?~~
3. Strategy and tactics
   ~~a. Method, medium, message worksheet~~
   b. SWOT analysis
   c. Strategic planning session, with discussion guide—conduct the session and report back to the class
~~4. Identifying volunteers~~
   ~~a. Database review and cleanup~~
   ~~b. Networking—you know someone who knows someone~~
   ~~c. Write a job description~~

Figure 4.3 Revised topic and activity outline for part of Marketing as a Mitzvah.

my communications classes is an online grammar review; on completing the mini-quiz, students can immediately see which items they got wrong, as well as an explanation of the grammar rule governing the situation. Although I also provide feedback on grammar rules once the student submits the results to me, the student receives immediate feedback right in the context of the activity itself.

Main topics, with activities for each topic:

1. What is marketing?
   a. List current tools and goal codes each
   b. Write volunteer job description as an exercise in internal marketing
   c. Identify and develop enhancement plan for one low-cost or no-cost marketing tactic
2. Strategy, then Tactics
   a. SWOT analysis
   b. Write an e-vite or web-based invitation
   c. Complete marketing planning worksheet
3. Understanding Audiences
   a. Level of commitment worksheet
   b. Information sleuth project—identify information repositories and come up with three new ways to use each
   c. Unaffiliated outreach—using levels worksheet to identify opportunities
4. Synagogue Re-orientation
   a. Write an internal communication plan—getting the synagogue on board with marketing
   b. Write an external communication plan—getting the community and seekers to know who you are
   c. Journal—how is this concept of marketing different from what you expected?

Figure 4.4 Final topic and activity outline for Marketing as a Mitzvah.

Got Tech?

If your list of activities involves anything of a technical nature (e.g., computer simulations, online surveys, interactive tools, etc.), now is the time to sit down with your guru and establish a time frame and specific budget for development. Depending on the complexity of your needs, development—including design, testing, and implementation—can take quite a while. Let it happen while you are working on other areas of your course content so that you don't create bottlenecks later in the process.

Core Content Development

With the activities established, I back up a little further. What information do participants need to complete the activity? Here is where I put the bulk of my time and energy—writing the lectures, finding the readings and resources, and lining up guest presenters—to provide students with the knowledge they need to learn. I call this portfolio of material the core content.

Core content may include audio or video materials, secondary sources, printed matter, presentations, lectures you will deliver via teleconference, and more. However, in my own courses, and in most of the distance-learning programs I have been involved with, core content tends to appear in the form of written lectures averaging between 500 and 1,500 words.

Tips for Writing Lectures

Writing lectures for distance learning is only nominally like writing lectures for traditional delivery. Distance-learning lectures are more than the delivery of core material; they are also the primary way students get to know the instructor. In a traditional classroom, students have a larger pool of data on which to make decisions about your competence; maybe your lectures are dense and convoluted, but you can really answer questions in a clear, cogent manner. Or you talk in a monotone but make up for it with fabulous multimedia presentations. On the other hand, in a distance-learning environment, if you bomb your lectures, you lose credibility, sink motivation, and make your entire job harder.

Telling Tales

The lessons of your lectures will make the most sense to students when they are embedded in real-world situations drawn from your own experiences. Use of narrative and anecdote to draw in the reader and illustrate the truth of your knowledge is an excellent way to engage students in the lecture material.

Lacking real-world experience in an area of study can be a stumbling block, but there are ways around it. Conduct and report on an interview with someone who has the experience; draw on mythology or allegory to illustrate your point; tell a story of a counterexample—a situation in which the target knowledge would have been helpful but wasn't present. Narrative is one of the fastest and easiest ways to get students emotionally and psychologically committed to learning what you present.

Short Sentences

If you do nothing else to your lectures, shorten the sentences. Subject, verb, predicate. In most cases, students will be reading your lectures on a computer screen, whether you deliver them via e-mail or within the context of a Web-based course platform. Long sentences are difficult to follow, particularly on a screen. It's a stylistic challenge to find ways to compress your sentences, but it pays off by enabling students to wrestle with the meat of your ideas rather than with convoluted clauses.

Structure for Motivation

Remember that motivation is critical to success, so build motivation right into your lectures and other written content. Students may well be printing out and referring to your lectures regularly, thinking about them, and carrying the content into other areas of their lives. You can use your lectures to motivate as well as instruct by structuring them to inspire students to keep going.

The following steps, when integrated into the flow of your documents, will spark and nurture motivation:

- **We are alike.** Motivational documents begin by establishing common ground between writer and reader. Make it clear that you can see the world from the students' perspective and that you've walked in their shoes.
- **Change is possible.** Bring home the idea that the status quo is not the only alternative. Remind students that the discomfort they feel in working with new ideas, skills, and concepts is the pain that accompanies growth.
- **The tools of change are available.** Immediately after reinforcing motivation by reminding students of the end-goal, present the main concepts—the tools of change.
- **The outcome will be satisfying.** Don't leave the reader without pushing the motivation button once more. Tell a story or demonstrate how a real positive impact can occur when someone just like them follows through with mastery of new skills.

The sample lecture from one of my communications courses, found in Appendix C, demonstrates how to apply this motivational structure to a written lecture.

Build on Core Content with Discussion and Activities

Since you are developing core content in direct relationship to the activities you've selected, you should find it relatively easy to draw direct links between lectures (or other core elements) and the activities. Place the instructions or an introduction to the activity right in the same location as the core content, and make the links explicit. Figure 4.5 shows an example of the end of a lecture and the start of an assignment for Marketing as a Mitzvah; this sample has the right amount of "bridging" information—perhaps more than you may think you need. Remember that you need to put in writing all the information you might otherwise clarify verbally. Even if you are using a synchronous meeting or event to deliver the content and then explain the assignment, put the extra information right in the documentation.

Data Activation

Research can only benefit you if you act on what you learn. Information in a file or in an individual's head is not actionable! Start to make the understanding and use of information a regular part of your discussions around synagogue events and how you plan.

You have new programs, new events, new audiences to reach, existing relationships that you could deepen? what information would make it easier to do so? Chances are, you already have in place a mechanism or tool for getting and using that information.

Assignment # 3-2: Info Sleuth

This assignment takes a bit of sleuthing at the synagogue. Your mission: discover the ways your synagogue collects *and uses* information. Make a list of all your information-gathering opportunities in a table like the following (create your own table, based on this model):

Information gathering	Frequency	How it is used
Membership database	Annually, and as new members join	Mailings and voting, primarily
Program evaluation	Following every program	Planning upcoming events and gathering ideas for new events

Now pick one of these information gathering opportunities to think through creatively. How could it work harder for you? How else might you apply the information you gather through this method? Is there an opportunity to go deeper with this tool by adding a component like a focus group or a survey? Do your evaluations need a bit of tweaking? Should you add some fields to your membership database?

Post your ideas on how you can enhance and leverage at least one existing information resource in the Discussion classroom in the thread titled "Assignment 3-2: Info Sleuth"

Figure 4.5 Bridge from lecture to activity for Marketing as a Mitzvah. *(Used with permission of STAR, www.starsynagogue.org, and JSkyway, www.jskway.com.)*

Lessons from the Copywriter

When I'm not doing one of the million other things in my professional life, I'm writing copy for a variety of professional uses. "Copy" was originally an advertising term referring to the written text that appears with any marketing material. These days, it's more common to hear writers speak about "developing content" than "writing copy," in part because advertising has a bad rap for being fluff, at best, and untrustworthy at worst.

I prefer the word "copy," however, because copy does something that content never can: Copy motivates a change in behavior, while content is static; content is about the topic, while copy is about the reader. The instructional structure for lectures is just one example of how your words do more than communicate course information. Remember that motivation is at the heart of successful distance-learning programs; write copy, not just content.

What does this mean in practical terms?

- **Use headings.** Especially for material designed to be read electronically, headings help break up the page and enable readers to identify key information. Readers tend to scan material, and headings force their eyeballs to slow down.
- **Short and sweet.** A two-column printed page can handle about 600 words without looking crowded. An e-mail preview pane displays approximately 10 lines of plain text. A standard Web screen looks clear and inviting with 200 to 400 words on it, depending on layout, typeface, and graphic elements.
- **Be real and accessible.** Work toward a written style that approximates your speaking voice (unless you are a naturally stuffy/uptight person; in that case, loosen up in your writing, and possibly in your life). Define words that your students might not be familiar with. Your writing should invite them in, not keep them out.
- **Involve the reader.** Use "you" and "your" and write as if you were having a one-on-one conversation with a specific person.

- **Tell a story.** Humans are highly story-oriented beings; narratives are a great way to reach their emotions and get them committed to learning the material.
- **Write in active voice.** Avoid "there is" and "there are" constructions.
- **Pare it down.** Say what you need to say using the fewest possible words.
- **Be specific.** Use examples from your own experience that your students will relate to. (This approach also helps you "be real.")
- **Remember to motivate.** Sometimes subtly, sometimes with a sledgehammer, motivate your students to push forward because of the outcome they want to achieve.
- **Get feedback.** Share written materials with several people, preferably with members of the target audiences, and ask them to highlight anything that doesn't work for them.

Want even more information on effective writing for distance-learning instruction? Visit the Web site for this book at www.electric-muse.com/tbyr.asp; register with a valid e-mail address, and you will receive a free white paper on writing tips and resources to use in crafting class materials and student communications.

Similarly, you will need to create discussion questions that build on the core content and make direct connections for students with their personal, practical experiences. Here, for example, is a sample discussion question from one of my introductory writing classes:

> Chapter 1 in *A Writer's Workshop* describes many different ideas and approaches to starting the writing process. Describe your own writing process—the steps you take when you sit down to complete a writing project. What works well for you? What would you like to change about your process? What is the hardest part for you? The easiest? What new ideas did you

get from reading this chapter about how you could change or enhance your own writing process?

Discussion built around students' personal experiences, linked with the concepts presented in the core content, provides opportunities for learners to reflect on their own experience within the context of the course materials. It also creates the potential for livelier discussion as students from different backgrounds and environments start to compare and contrast their experiences.

Instructional Events

Written lectures need to move readers through the events of instruction and prepare them to engage in the next event through activities. Lectures and other core content are the natural place to gain attention, inform the student about objectives, stimulate prior recall, and present content. When these elements are linked with activities and followed up with individual and group feedback, reflection, and synthesis, they carry the learner all the way through the instructional process.

Waiting for the Movie Release?

Occasionally, I am asked whether it is preferable to create an audiovisual version of a lecture for online delivery, or even whether instructors should have themselves filmed delivering a lecture and then use the recording for an online lecture. Certainly the possibility of using video and audio versions of a lecture has become more viable in the past few years, via both Web-based delivery and stand-alone media such as CDs or DVDs.

My advice is to be cautious in your use of audio or video for lectures. In addition to the increased costs and complexity, it is much more difficult to edit, change, or adapt material that has been packaged in a technology-dependent format. From the students' perspective, too, use of audio or video requires them to have access to the technology at the time they want to interact with the material; unlike a written lecture, which they can print and review at their leisure, an audiovisual lecture requires them to be at the delivery system (e.g., computer, DVD player, broadband terminal, etc.) and to take notes.

However, there are times when audiovisual materials are truly a preferred solution. One company implemented a training program structured around taped lectures for its on-the-road sales force. Salespeople could listen to the tapes in their cars while driving from customer to customer. In that case, a text-dependent option would have been less functional and portable for the audience.

Still, it's usually best to come up with uses for audio and video that are more strategic and less cumbersome for the user. For example, one instructor I know uses a personal minibiopic as a form of introduction. As part of her standard course materials, she includes a 2-minute "talking heads" interview, a few family photos, and her personal statement about the joy of teaching. She doesn't need to update the material very often, so she gets the value of her development investment, and her students enjoy having this tech-driven opportunity to get to know her. Other appropriate applications include field videos, interview excerpts (no more than 5 to 7 minutes), archival video or film, and audio recordings of music or native speakers (for foreign language instruction). Certainly students who can't be present at a live Web event or teleconference will appreciate having the archived version available, especially if it has search functions and the capability to submit follow-up questions to the presenter.

Challenges Unique to Distance Instruction

Much of the information presented so far would actually be just as helpful in preparing a traditional course as it is in preparing a distance-learning program. Many of us who are instructors never received formal training in instruction. Having a process for identifying what to cover, how to structure assignments, and how to pace the progress provides us with a method for something we've been doing largely by instinct. An ability to write for both instruction and motivation can be invaluable, even if you are delivering lectures in person rather than at a distance. An emphasis on practical activities and learner needs helps us move beyond our expertise to focus on the experience of the students.

Yet distance learning does create its own requirements for content development. The rest of this chapter will lay out the special issues and opportunities associated with creating distance-learning instructional materials.

The Expectation of Interactivity

In the Introduction, I said it plainly: The core of learning is interaction. In creating materials for distance-learning instruction, you have to build the expectation of interactivity directly into the content itself.

What does interactivity really mean? "Click here" is not interactive, any more than turning the page of a textbook is interactive. Materials that are interactive change when a learner touches them. They're even more effective when they require learners to employ higher thinking to get the result they expect out of the interaction.

Getting students to be involved with their learning is the secret of success. When you create materials that raise the expectation of interactivity, you are setting the stage for them to be involved and committed to further involvement.

A simple yet effective model of interactive course material is a study guide that requires the user to complete the blanks in a series of sentences based on information found in the readings or lectures. By writing down the information, students are forced to incorporate it bodily and visually.

Simulations and games are also great forms of interactivity, although they can be expensive and time consuming to create. Similarly, and less expensively, online surveys or polling systems can engage learners and at the same time provide them with food for thought. For example, a particular leadership development program used an online survey made up of "yes/no" questions on muddy topics in ethics, fundraising, and nonprofit management. The participants were forced to select "yes" or "no" for situations that were definite "maybes." When they completed the survey, they were able to view the aggregated responses of the entire class; what followed was a series of highly engaged discussions in the classroom as the participants struggled together over the issues. Because of the way they had already interacted with the material, the participants turned what could have been a theoretical discussion into a highly personal one.

Single-Purpose Documents

The complete and unabridged syllabus (which we'll write before finishing this chapter) is the North Star for any course. With all the information relating to performance, deadlines, topics, assignments, and course policies in one place, I have a single place to direct students when problems or questions arise. However, as a communication tool, a syllabus of

50+ pages is unwieldy. Much of the most important information, including participation requirements, deadlines, major projects, and Netiquette policies, I also provide in stand-alone, single-purpose documents.

Single-purpose documents are easier for students (and instructors) to find when needed. They're also easier to absorb. Apply this concept to other forms of your communication with students; if you mail or e-mail instructions, keep the communication to three or four items at most. Find other tools within your learning environment (posting classroom announcements? your signature line in e-mail communications?) to vary the ways you communicate with students. Variety, coupled with single-purpose documents, keeps students from tuning you out.

Repetition, Repetition, Repetition

"The assignment and the deadline were clearly listed in the syllabus. How come no one seemed to know how to do the project or when it was due?"

You will need to repeat information and instructions in a distance-learning environment far more often than you might think necessary. For most of my classes, I include all assignment information right in the syllabus; I also highlight assignments in a weekly posting of "What's New." A major or complex assignment will also be detailed in a stand-alone resource document, sometimes complete with FAQs. And I still expect to get several clarifying (or even totally clueless) questions from students.

Why the repetition? Can't they read the syllabus?

Consider a traditional classroom with a term paper due midway through the course:

- The instructor puts basic information about the assignment in the syllabus.
- In the first class meeting, a student asks about major assignments for the course, creating an opportunity to highlight the assignment and talk about its requirements.
- During class discussion, a student mentions a topic she is considering for her paper. The instructor comments on the topic and reiterates the timeline for completion.
- Some weeks before the assignment is due, the instructor devotes class time to elaborating on the project and soliciting questions.

- A student e-mails the instructor with a question about another assignment; the instructor responds and also asks how research for the term paper is progressing.

That's a lot of repetition, with a lot of opportunities for give-and-take between instructor and students to clarify goals and requirements. An instructor has to create the same kinds of opportunities for repetition in a distance-learning environment, taking into account that, in contrast with a traditional classroom, a good portion of the distribution of information will take place either (1) in writing (and digitally delivered writing at that) or (2) over the phone, reducing the points of input in the exchange. You can't see the eye-rolling, the glazed expressions, and the naked panic. You have to find other ways to capture that kind of data about your learners so that you can help them.

Nonlinear Approaches

Distance-learning programs enable students to enter and move through the material in unexpected ways. Depending on the degree to which you want to encourage this kind of experimentation (with some audiences, you don't really have a choice; Millennials will do it no matter what you tell them), you need to keep student navigational behavior in mind when you create your content.

For example, be sure that key terms are always defined the first time they appear in *any* course document, not just what you think of as the *first* appearance. (You can minimize the hassle of this requirement, at least in an online environment, by linking key terms to a glossary database. That way, no matter where the students find the term, they can look up its meaning, if necessary.)

Thinking about your information in a nonlinear fashion is a bit of a mental trick at first. After writing Web sites for many years, I do it almost unconsciously. I remember that when I was learning how to do it I found it helpful to print out and shuffle my content, pick up a section at random, and see if I could locate myself within the material. If I had trouble, I knew that it was still too linear. I would rewrite the section so that a user entering at that point would be able to make an informed decision about what to do next.

For most of my courses, I separate content into weekly modules that build on one another in a decidedly linear manner. Within each module, though, I aim to make each component stand on its own. I have a preferred path through the material, but a learner who chooses a different path, for whatever reason, will still be able to complete the work.

Customizable Pathways

Similar to nonlinear content, customizable pathways through the content enable learners with different learning styles, interests, and backgrounds to create the most effective learning experience possible. I often create two or more forms of an activity or an assignment—one that is largely text-based (remember, I'm a writer and a verbal learner) and the others to appeal to learners who prefer other kinds of activities. Since I've asked students to complete a learning style self-assessment, they are equipped to pick the option that best suits their preferred style.

Another way to create customizable pathways is by a learner's background or existing skill set. My communications classes and my creative writing classes mix English-as-a-second-language (ESL) students with native speakers. I've learned to develop additional materials and resources for ESL students so they can tackle the material regardless of the level of their language skills.

Marketing as a Mitzvah also has a subtle element of learner-based customization. The learners in this course are organized into teams of three individuals from each participating synagogue, usually a rabbi, a staff member, and a volunteer. Several activities and discussion topics are geared specifically for each type of participant—for instance, a reflective journal for the rabbi, a marketing-budget project for the staff member, and a resource-development challenge for the volunteer. This approach allows everyone to get what is most personally and professionally relevant from the course while remaining in the same workshop environment.

Reusable Learning Objects

Once you've started teaching a few distance-learning offerings, you may find that some introductory elements of your courses are more or less the same, regardless of the medium or the type of course you are teaching. Make life easier by creating your own library of reusable learning objects. For instance, my "getting started with distance learning" document rarely changes, regardless of the particular offering; I almost always have at least a few students who are new to distance learning, and even those who have participated in distance-learning offerings benefit from this introduction, which lays out *my* expectations for participation, assignments, etc. (A copy of my "getting started" document is included with the other sample materials in Appendix B.) Similarly, my Netiquette document is the same for every online course I offer. As you prepare classes, consider which of the materials you are developing may be applicable with few or no changes to additional courses.

Distance learning—no matter what blend of tools you are using to pull it off—requires a great deal of written documentation to be successful. The written word becomes the primary connection among instructor, content, and students, whether it's an e-mailed assignment, a syllabus, or the contents of an online lecture or presentation. The words you use, your style, even the layout of your pages or screens will make a difference in how well you bridge the distance between instructor and class.

Course Content RLOs

In addition to reusable introductory materials, you may find that you can reuse portions of your core content portfolio for other courses. But be cautious of adopting an overly "cut and paste" approach to reusable learning objects (RLOs). Course content created for one type of situation may not be directly applicable to another situation; if you change the types of learners, the medium of interaction, or the goals of the program, the content might need to be completely rewritten to satisfy the new requirements.

Even if you can't reuse course content (your own or that provided by a course library), you can save yourself a lot of time by adapting rather than starting from scratch. Evaluate course material for its reuse potential and enjoy the savings in time and cost that reuse can afford you. But don't be surprised if even small changes in the audience or desired outcomes for a course demand significant shifts in the presentation of content.

Special Considerations for E-Learning

"The Web may be the worst thing that could have happened to distance learning," e-learning guru Michael Allen told me. "Eventually, it will be the best thing that could have happened, but for now, it's resulting in a lot of poor instruction. Developers are putting stuff up on the Web that doesn't work for instruction and learning." Whether the Web represents the best or the worst of distance learning, it's clear that e-learning has important specific requirements regarding content development.

Visual Content

The Web is a powerfully visual medium, yet too often content is text oriented. Reading Web-based text is tiring for the eyeballs and results in lowered concentration and reduced retention of the information. If your users need to scroll more than two pages' worth of material, you need to break it up into additional pages.

Online readers naturally scan material rather than reading every word. Write, design, and implement Web-based material that students can scan for key information and read more closely later to fully understand. Use of headlines, icons, and other elements that stop the scanning eyeball will give readers visual clues about where and how to enter and work with your content.

Screen Design

"Keep it simple" is a good motto for creating Web-based classroom experiences. Overloading the page with information, action elements, graphics, and options actually taxes the learner's short-term memory and thus can negatively affect performance and retention.

Use a good-sized font, colors that are easy to view, and a consistent layout for each page within your course. If users are squinting to read the material or trying to reorient themselves every time they view a different page, they will become impatient and dissatisfied with the experience.

Presentations

The temptation is always present: Just take your presentations, which you've lovingly developed and delivered to rave reviews, and put them on the Web: instant content!

Nope. It doesn't work. Presentations are not the same as Web-based learning materials. Wholesale copying from presentation to Web is like filming an actor reading a novel out loud and calling it a movie version of the book. Content created for one medium needs to be adapted and changed to succeed in another.

If you are tempted to create or reuse presentations for Web-based courses, consider instead what the learning outcome of that particular component is. Usually there's a more elegant way to achieve it than by inserting something created for another environment.

Web-Based Resources

Any class can incorporate Web-based resources into the learning experience, but e-learning programs have a unique opportunity to make the Web into a virtual library, field trip, and scavenger hunt. The use of live links, online resource collections, and other Web components can make your online classroom reach beyond itself. As you incorporate these elements, be mindful of copyright implications; for more information on copyright within a distance-learning program, see Appendix D.

Working with Tools

Course management systems like Blackboard and WebCT are designed to make it easy for online instructors to create, implement, and manage feature-rich distance-learning courses. These environments offer variety, robust tools, references, and course materials. They also involve steep learning curves. When you teach on a course management system—particularly the first few times—allow extra time to learn how to master all those controls and options, not to mention to get your materials uploaded to the tool, proofread, and tested.

It's also a good idea to create a learner's guide to the platform itself so that incoming students have a useful, course-specific reference to the features and applications within the system. The platform vendor may have a guide you can customize, so be sure to ask.

High Time for Collaboration

"Do what you do best and hire the rest." This is a basic survival technique of independent professionals. Sure, I *could* learn HTML and database management on top of developing, marketing, and teaching my courses, but when would I have time to do my other work, sleep, exercise, enjoy my family, and take the occasional nap?

When implementing a Web-based course, I always work with others who help me create content, think through the right Web-based solution for a pedagogical challenge, and get beyond my own experience so that I can better serve students. Some areas I simply don't have interest in pursuing; some I doubt I could ever be good at, even if I had all the time in the world to put into them. I'm fortunate to work with great professionals who care as much about software, Web development, and course management as I do about teaching. Although collaboration can add yet another layer of complexity to a project, it always results in a better outcome.

Take a Deep Breath and Jump

You will never be truly, entirely ready to create your first distance-learning course. At some point, you have to simply take a deep breath and jump in.

By this point, your brain may by overloaded with plans, ideas, and questions. Take your topic syllabus and revise it based on what you actually created for content. Then fill in the rest of the syllabus to create the document that will serve as the contract between you and your students. Lay out exactly what you expect and what they can expect of you. It will be frighteningly long, and it will take about twice as long as you expect the first time you do it, but a comprehensive syllabus is a cornerstone of creating an environment of trust and clarity for you and your students. Worksheet 4.1 provides a framework through which you can create your syllabus.

Worksheet 4.1 Complete Syllabus

Complete this syllabus worksheet to be sure you are covering all the critical areas for a distance-learning syllabus.

I. Administrative Information

Course Name:
Schedule:
Dates:
Synchronous sessions:
Asynchronous access:
Instructor:
Contact information: (e-mail) (phone)
Availability (include time zone):
Alternative contacts:
Prerequisites:
Required reading:
Required resources:
Baseline technology:

II. Course Description

Narrative description:
Topics:
Learning objectives:
Successful outcomes:

III. Grading and Evaluation

Criteria:
Expectations for returning feedback:
Calendar for due dates:

IV. Course Policies

Class access:
Attendance:
Participation:
Netiquette:
Acceptable formats:
Late assignments:
Feedback:
Plagiarism statement:
Privacy statement:
Grievance procedures:

V. Group Work

Creation of working groups:
Group project requirements:

Worksheet 4.1 (cont.)

VI. Detailed Topics and Activities

[Create a section of the syllabus for each of your topic areas]

Topic:
Objectives:
Reading and prework:
Individual assignments:
    Activity descriptions and due dates:
    Instructions for completion and submission:
Group assignments:
    Activity descriptions and due dates:
    Instructions for completion and submission:

Summary of Deliverables for Topic:

Individual/Group	What?	Where?	When?
Indicate individual or group work	*Deliverable element*	*Where should students put completed work?*	*Deadline for full credit*

Beta Testing

Just because you're jumping in doesn't mean you have to do it without a life jacket. Find ways to test and validate the course you've worked so hard to develop before bringing in the students. Invite a recent student and a prospective student to review the course and provide feedback. Recent learners are still in touch with what they enjoyed about their experience as well as what they wish it had included. Prospective learners are the true test case—the ones who will let you know if what you've created will work for your target students.

Sometimes testing isn't possible, of course—you'll always run into situations with impossible deadlines. Your first students may also be your "beta testers." As you teach a course, especially the first time, keep handy some working versions of all your content so that you can make notes regarding what you want to change or enhance the next time around.

Budgeting Time

How much time does it take to prepare a distance-learning class? This is always one of the first questions I'm asked when I talking with a new or prospective distance-learning instructor. The answer, of course, is "it depends." It depends on the format of the course, how much content you are covering, the expectations of the students coming into the course, the kind of delivery system you are using, the amount of existing material you can reuse and revise, and how much time you have, since projects will almost always expand to fill whatever space you give them on your calendar.

There's no doubt that preparing for a distance-learning course takes more time than preparing for a traditional course, even if you are using low-tech or no-tech approaches to delivery. The checklist in Worksheet 4.2 may look a bit daunting, but it will help you organize your time and effort throughout course preparation.

On the up side, however, all this preparation pays off by freeing up your attention in the classroom so that you can focus on the students. In a traditional class, I'm lecturing and leading discussion; I'm thinking as much about what I need to say next (and hoping I don't forget anything) as I am about what the students need. In distance-learning programs, by the time I get into the "classroom," I've already said what I need to say; I can devote all my energy and attention to interacting with students, guiding them to the materials they need most, engaging them, motivating them, and responding to their questions and insights.

And that makes a great segue into the next chapter—what an instructor needs to do to actively manage the distance "classroom," encouraging and guiding the learning process for the students.

Worksheet 4.2 Course Content Development Checklist

- ☐ Complete instructional design process (Chapter 3)
- ☐ Draft topic syllabus (Chapter 3)
  - ☐ List potential activities for each topic (Chapter 3)
- ☐ Refine learning goals for course—what does success look like?
- ☐ Refine learning objectives
- ☐ Refine topic list
- ☐ Select and develop culminating activity for course
  - ☐ What do students need to be able to do before they can do that activity?
  - ☐ Select and develop "stepping-stone" activities
  - ☐ Make final list of 1 to 3 activities in each topic area
  - ☐ Cover range of learning styles with activities—check for the following:
    - ☐ Verbal activities
    - ☐ Visual activities
    - ☐ Kinesthetic activities
    - ☐ Aural activities
    - ☐ Social activities
    - ☐ Solitary activities
    - ☐ Logical activities
  - ☐ Compare to learning objectives
- ☐ What do students need to know in order to be able to complete this activity?
- ☐ Develop core content
  - ☐ Write lectures
  - ☐ Discuss multimedia and Web-based tools with collaborative partners
  - ☐ Develop timeline and budgets for materials that need to be developed externally
  - ☐ Identify other resources
    - ☐ Library
    - ☐ Web materials
    - ☐ Books
    - ☐ Articles
    - ☐ Guest speakers
    - ☐ Video
    - ☐ Audio
    - ☐ Other
- ☐ Write activity instructions and bridging material
- ☐ Evaluate content for nonlinear pathways and customization potential
- ☐ Write detailed syllabus, including final topics, activities, assignments, and policy information
- ☐ Write or pull and adapt standard and stand-alone documentation (e.g., welcome, netiquette, participation requirements, learning team instructions, etc.)
- ☐ Implement content (e.g., design and lay out, upload to Web platform, create digital files, etc.)
- ☐ Proofread and test content
- ☐ Review course for consistency, tone, usability
- ☐ Test with students, if possible

Chapter 5

Time to Go to Class

What does it mean to manage a classroom within the context of distance learning? It's as critical in distance learning as it is in a traditional classroom for an instructor to maintain gentle (and at times forceful) control over the formal learning environment. Perhaps even more so: Distance-learning students are looking to their instructors to create order from what appears to be chaos and to help them feel as connected as they do in traditional classrooms. They too are comparing distance learning to an expected norm. How the instructor manages their classroom experience makes an enormous difference in their willingness and ability to learn in a new environment.

But what are the parameters of a classroom when instructors and students are out of earshot? Where is it located? What are its requirements and character? The following definition is a helpful starting point for thinking about the instructor's role in the classroom, regardless of the medium of the course:

> **Definition of the Classroom:** The classroom is the designated space in which all three of the critical interactions of learning take place: interaction with peers, content, and instructor. The classroom is under the guidance and authority of the instructor, who is responsible for creating a culture of learning and exchange, risk-taking, inquiry, and collaboration, as well as setting and communicating the criteria for successful performance.

Some forms of distance learning (such as self-paced, self-contained training programs, tutorials, and the like) do not involve a classroom; they may involve instructors who respond individually to a student's input, but they do not require the instructor to manage the activity in a classroom environment. For such programs to have much depth or value beyond the development of discrete skill sets, however, requires extraordinary expense. In most cases, the cost-effective solution in which students need to expand beyond their own experience, think critically, and master concepts as well as skills is to create a classroom environment of some type—even a simple listserv, live Webinar, or discussion board—and make it a central component of the distance-learning program. Whenever that environment is implemented, an instructor needs to know how to manage it and maximize its instructional value.

One of the most common misconceptions and concerns of prospective distance-learning students is that their experience will be impoverished by minimal contact with an instructor. Yet instructor contact can be more intimate and rewarding in a distance-learning environment than in a traditional environment, provided the instructor understands how to use the classroom to connect one-on-one as well as with the group.

Instructors too may have erroneous beliefs about distance-learning classrooms. They may mistakenly believe that distance learning requires little skill in classroom management. Especially in the wake of the hours of preparation before launching a course, instructors may expect (or at least hope) that the classroom can largely run itself. Early efforts in computer-mediated education tried to move in that direction, but the results were disappointingly poor learning experiences for students. Guess what? We instructors are needed!

The classroom opportunity for interchange with a living, breathing instructor allows students to grapple on a deeper level with the content of a course. The give-and-take between instructor and student offers the teaching moments when a good instructor can open up an entirely new way of thinking for a student.

The idea of give-and-take is critical: Interaction between student and instructor means that you too will be learning from the exchange. This learning might help you make enhancements to your course materials, or it may suggest a whole new area of study in which to begin developing a distance-learning program. Interaction will have a resounding impact on how you teach, what you teach, and even why you teach.

What follows are key tips and best practices for managing the distance-learning environment.

Predictability

Can you imagine how confusing it would be if your traditional class met in a different location every session and each location had a radically different atmosphere? If you met one week in a comfy coffee shop and the next in a sterile lab, what kind of expectations would you be creating for your students? Or imagine how your students would react if during one class session you were gregarious and outgoing, and the next you sat in stony, unblinking silence. They'd probably clam up, waiting for more predictable cues from you as to what you were seeking.

Predictability creates the necessary conditions for learning and exchange. Without it, your students will put their creative and intellectual energy into figuring out your expectations rather than mastering the material. Until students trust you, they are unteachable, and trust is predicated on predictability.

You can create predictability in a number of ways. Detailed, sensible policies set out at the start of a class (about participation, deadlines, and other requirements) create predictability. The tone of your documents, the look and feel of materials, and even the organization of the course documentation itself are specific areas to focus on the consistency of your messages. Does the font suddenly change from Times New Roman to Arial? Do the colors used in your classroom Web page change from day to day and page to page, without rhyme or reason? Students may not even consciously notice these differences, yet they accumulate in the students' "perception banks." They delay the process by which students get to know the learning environment and settle down to the work of learning. In your final edits (as noted in Worksheet 4.2, at the end of Chapter 4), hunt down inconsistencies in the execution of your course content.

Once in the classroom, have and communicate a relatively predictable schedule for your own availability and involvement in the course. If you are highly visible and chatty for 3 or 4 days of asynchronous discussion and then disappear without a trace for a week, your students won't know what to expect of you or what you truly expect of them. Certainly emergencies come up, but when they do, you need to communicate with your students about what they can expect from you for the relationship—and the classroom—to work.

Life Happens

A couple of summers ago, when I was working on weekly feedback for the students in a communications course, I went out early in the evening to walk down to the local convenience store. My daughter and I had our taste buds set for ice cream. Somehow, stepping off the curb into the street, I twisted my foot badly. Despite the shooting pain, I limped down the block to fulfill our cravings before limping home.

Within an hour, the pain had intensified, and I was sure I had managed to break something. During 2 hours in the urgent care waiting room, I graded a few papers; 2 hours later, I was home, icing a bad sprain.

Knowing that there was no way I could get detailed feedback to students by my usual deadline, I posted a message to them in the classroom:

> Subject: A funny thing happened on the way to the ice cream shop …
>
> Just when you think you've mastered the art of walking, a curb jumps in your face and trips you up. I'm back from several hours at the urgent care, with my ankle tightly wrapped and a pile of half-graded papers next to me on the couch. Please know that I am working as quickly as I can to complete feedback and grading on last week's work, but I will not be able to return it to you for another 24 hours. I will also be absent from the classroom during this period so that I can focus on feedback. My apologies …
>
> P.S. We still managed to get to the ice cream shop and back; a girl's gotta have priorities!

The students appreciated the note explaining the delay, as well as the humanness of my message to them. Even the class renegade dropped me a note to let me know he understood my predicament. I met my new deadline without compromising the quality of the feedback.

Even within predictability, you have room to be flexible with your own schedule; some weeks you might feel like managing the classroom at 2 A.M. (Insomnia? Just fed the baby?) rather than at your typical 10 A.M. time slot. Just be sure your students know about the shift so that they can adapt.

Be Prepared

More than half of this book concerns preparations for your distance-learning classroom, and that's not accidental. Distance instruction requires hours of preparation time. Still, in the classroom itself, you have to be prepared. Know your syllabus, your resources, and how to access your support system. Students will have questions about where to find materials and assignments, how to contact technical support, and where to find information for that assignment due next week (or the one due yesterday). Good familiarity with the nuts and bolts of the course will help you respond quickly so that you can all get back to learning.

If you recently developed the course you are about to teach, preparation is pretty simple since it's all fresh. However, if you are teaching a course that someone else developed, or if you are dusting off a course you haven't taught in a while, take time before the students show up to familiarize yourself with its requirements and components.

It's also a good idea to have someone else prepared to take over if needed. After years of self-employment, I've learned to have backup coverage for time-sensitive and critical projects. What happens to your class if, heaven forbid, you have an intimate encounter with the radiator grille of a school bus? It's like writing a will—no one wants to imagine *what if*, but you owe it to your students and your classroom to consider what options you have available if you are put out of commission during a course period.

Plan for the Inevitable

If you are using technology to deliver your course, know this: Something will not work as expected. It might be as minor as losing access to e-mail for an hour or two. It might be as major as a series of hurricanes blowing out all the phone and Internet connections for your 10 students on the Atlantic Coast (been there, done that). It might even be something internal to the course: a bug that goes undetected in courseware until you suddenly have 50 students trying to access an activity. When technology is involved, even the most redundant systems can fail.

You have to think on your feet in a distance classroom, just as you would in a traditional one. When disruptions of this nature occur, your No. 1 resource is always your creativity and good humor. Screaming at the monitor will not solve the problem. Screaming at your Web developer will only cause an entirely different set of problems. Don't get mad; get creative. You may need to

- Resort to faxing or snail-mailing materials that were supposed to be available via e-mail or the Web.
- Extend deadlines or even the length of the course.
- Accept alternative, equivalent work from students. For example, you might allow them to complete a group project individually or turn an individual project into a team effort.
- Substitute different activities and learning experiences for the ones you had planned. For instance, turn an online research project into one students can complete at a brick-and-mortar library.

For your own sanity and the smooth operation of your classroom, find a way to manage the technical hiccups without losing your sense of perspective or your temper.

Train the Students to Your Expectations

Because distance learning is a new environment for so many students, instructors need to attend to some basic training and handholding about expectations in the classroom. Before launching a class, be sure your policy documents and class guidelines are clear and comprehensive. Everything—including Netiquette, assignments, deadlines, participation, and more—should be laid out in both your syllabus and stand-alone documents.

It's not enough to simply give students these resources and documents, however. Chances are a quarter of your students will read them thoroughly, half will skim them, and the rest will ignore them entirely. Although my participation guidelines are described in my syllabi, detailed in stand-alone documents, and reiterated in the first few days in the classroom, I still have students who are surprised when I inform them that they haven't met the minimum requirements. Training students to understand and perform to your expectations requires a bit of creativity and persistence. Here are some methods you can try:

- **Helpful hints messages.** Incorporate an opportunity to provide brief instruction about some element of classroom life in a posting, an e-mail, or prior to leading a conference call session. For example, when I led a recent conference call component of a professional training program, I started with a brief reminder of how to access our online asynchronous discussion and asked two students who had been successful with the tool to comment on their experience (a nifty bit of peer-to-peer coaching and group bonding). For some classes, I include a statement in the "signature block" of my e-mail messages that will help them with the course (see Figure 5.1).
- **Syllabus quiz.** Some instructors create a brief quiz on policies and syllabus guidelines for students to complete at the start of a course. The quiz, while fairly simple, reiterates the importance of the information in what is essentially a contract between instructor and student regarding the requirements and expectations of the course.
- **Introductory assignment.** Like the syllabus quiz, an introductory assignment helps students master the volumes of new information involved when participating in a distance-learning class by incorporating knowledge of policies into an actual course assignment. This approach works more or less well, depending on the topic of the course. For instance, it works very well with my courses in written communication, in which I assign a short paper on Netiquette as one of the first assignments. By completing the assignment, students are forced to review Netiquette policies for the course and reflect on their own contribution to a respectful, engaging environment.

Robin Neidorf
Electric Muse: Information. Inspiration. Communication.
robin@electric-muse.com
Have something to say. Say it effectively.
====================================
Classroom tip: Use "Reply All" to respond to everyone;
use "Reply" to respond only to original sender;
trim the original message to clarify the part you are responding to.

Figure 5.1 A signature block I've used for e-mail communication in distance-learning courses. Under my contact information, students can find a tip about using the classroom. I rotate the message every few days to cover a range of tips I want them to have.

What all these approaches have in common is that they involve "push" communication (instructor effort to bring critical information to the students) rather than relying on "pull" communication (static documents that students have to find on their own). The use of push in addition to pull enables the instructor to guide the students through the mountains of material to those items that make an immediate difference in the functionality of the classroom.

Be Responsive

Especially at the start of a distance-learning course, students are likely to be overwhelmed by the new environment. They are absorbing a great deal of information in a very short time, and they are making new discoveries about their own preferences, needs, and biases in the process. Work with them to help them understand how to maximize their use of the distance classroom, and listen to their concerns. I make a point of monitoring classroom activity very closely at first, checking an asynchronous classroom every few hours and interrupting my own progress in a synchronous classroom every few minutes to see if I've lost or confused anyone.

In the first few classroom encounters, expect a lot of Help! and SOS! messages, which will need immediate attention to put your students at ease. Your immediate response, even if you can't solve the problem, will go a long way in helping skittish students relax.

At the online campus of the University of Phoenix, students need to access learning materials via the secure Web site as well as through our newsgroup classroom. Sometimes, especially in high-volume periods right after new courses are launched, the site is slow or even inaccessible. Particularly with new students who are still trying to find their way around, unavailable pages cause great anxiety; the students are convinced they are doing something utterly wrong. I can respond to their fear by reassuring them, "It's not you; it's the system. It does this at the start of a class when everyone's trying to access it at once." My reassurance doesn't solve the problem, but it does help students feel less in the dark about their learning environment.

Of course, sometimes you *can* solve the problem right away, which makes everyone feel better. I frequently coach students who are confused because they can't see their own postings to a classroom, listserv, or forum. When I can talk them through ways to refresh their display or change their default settings so that they can see their own messages, they are delighted and reassured.

Beyond technical glitches (some of which are user induced and others of which are truly technical), you'll find that responsiveness also helps in the ongoing struggle to encourage participation. In the early stages of any distance-learning program, I am in close contact with any students who seem to be struggling with participation or are altogether invisible. The student who seems to be lurking on the teleconference or in the Webinar will get a quick e-mail or phone call to learn more about his or her needs. The student whose messages come through with a particular tone of desperation will get a soothing e-mail pointing out his or her successes to date and suggesting a few ways to make the acclimation process easier.

As I respond, coach, and interact with new students, I'm careful to use their posting errors as a teaching opportunity rather than a chance to show them who holds the grade book around here and "ding" them. (As a course continues, I expect them to overcome the learning curve, and I'm less likely to forgive consistent and egregious errors.) The student who never posts comments in the right place gets a bit of gentle instruction, both inside and outside the classroom. The student who submits the first assignment a few hours late gets a brief "Everything

OK?" message rather than an immediate reduction in points; that way, I can gather information about the particular kind of coaching a student may need to be successful.

By consistently managing the classroom this way, you demonstrate to the students your professional care of them, as their instructor. They will come to trust you more readily because they will perceive you as a partner in their learning process rather than an adversary—a revelation for many adults, who may have had few nurturing relationships with their teachers if any.

Points for Participation

Participation is one area in which I continually work to train students to my expectations. (Do I seem obsessed with participation?) In distance learning, participation requires conscious skill development in an area students previously have taken for granted—raising their hands and making a comment.

A common challenge is to route students' participation to the classroom rather than let them fall into the habit of directing personal communication to me. Part of the problem is that, in addition to the fear of looking like a fool in the public space, new students do not yet understand how their classroom participation co-creates the learning experience, for themselves and for their classmates. If their primary educational model has been test-and-tell, they are not prepared for active involvement in or responsibility for their role in the classroom.

Their course-related questions, in particular, tend to show up in my e-mail inbox until I can train them otherwise. In asynchronous classrooms, I keep an active "questions here!" thread throughout the course, and in synchronous classrooms, I am careful to break up meeting times with solicitations of questions. Still, even with prodding and encouragement, I get many questions e-mailed privately or phoned in. If I responded privately, then the rest of the class would not benefit from the questions or have an opportunity to come up with alternative solutions to the ones I present.

When I receive private questions that relate to the course, I present them within the activity of the classroom. In an asynchronous classroom, for example, I post my own message to the thread for questions, beginning with something along the lines of "Several students have contacted me privately about research for their final projects ..." In a synchronous environment, I do something similar during the designated Q&A time: "I can't remember who came to me with this question, but it seemed like something that we should discuss together."

In reality, I may have received only one private question—or none at all. But the posting or the statement never fails to encourage follow-up questions. It's a handy trick for training the students to be more open about asking for guidance and clarification about what they don't know, and it reminds them that they are not penalized for asking questions and thus admitting ignorance.

On the flip side, I sometimes also have to train students to recognize that the classroom isn't the appropriate place for every discussion. Off-topic dialogues, while a welcome part of the community-building process, can make a distance-learning classroom confusing and chaotic. Many times I've had to interrupt an online discussion thread with a brief "How about taking this to the chat room, guys?" or suggest during a teleconference that a particular line of questioning would make a great team project that can be discussed privately.

Hold Office Hours

At least once a week, perhaps more frequently in a very short course or as circumstances warrant, make yourself available to your students only via phone, e-mail, and instant messaging (IM). Let them know the day and time (including time zone) you are holding office hours. If you will be unable to hold your regular hours, schedule an alternative time.

Foster Dialogue

The classroom is the natural place to stimulate recall of prior learning, present content, practice and encode skills, assess performance, and exchange feedback—many of the necessary events of instruction. It all takes place through discussion and dialogue among classmates as well as between instructor and student.

Dialogue means more than people talking to each other or posting messages in the classroom space. Rather, dialogue is an interchange that deepens ideas and awareness and is truly more than the sum of its parts. Dialogue requires conscious nurturing even more than it requires basic participation. (And you already know how I feel about participation.)

Keeping in mind the characteristics of adult students can be helpful in figuring out how to foster dialogue among them. Adult students bring their experiences into the classroom, and they learn best when they can apply what they are learning to their own world. Some ways to foster dialogue include the following:

- Build on contributions by sharing your own expertise and insight.
- Invite students to provide illustrative or contrasting examples from their own experiences.
- Relate a comment to the core content, or draw a connection between the comment and a new resource.
- Compare and contrast contributions from multiple students.

When a student adds to the richness of the dialogue, follow up in the classroom with praise, by identifying the specific way the student added depth and meaning. This practice helps others learn what you are looking for. It also provides positive reinforcement and public recognition for quality contributions. Similarly, encourage students whose responses are scanty to probe more deeply by using examples from their work and life that support their ideas.

Repeat Yourself

I've mentioned the value of repeating information and instructions several times. Classroom management also benefits from repeating yourself. (What do you know—I'm repeating it!)

No matter how clearly you give instructions for an assignment, someone will have a question. And truthfully, we're not always quite as clear in our instructions as we think we are. Use the classroom environment to reiterate critical information, such as due dates, where to find the glossary or the class roster when necessary, or your availability for private consultation. It can be subtle, like a breezily added comment: "This is a great idea to incorporate into the paper you're working on for next week."

There's also value in repeating the same kind of feedback and critique if you have several students who are making common errors in the classroom. I run into this situation regularly in my asynchronous writing classes, in which many students share the same difficulties with grammar (pronouns in particular give us all grief). Sometimes it feels as if I'm making the same comments over and over ("A singular noun requires a singular pronoun: *his or her* rather than *their* ..."), but the repetition is good for everyone. For one thing, if I comment publicly on the error only the first few times it crops up in student posts, those few students may feel picked on, so I point it out continuously. But more importantly, many students only read carefully the responses I make to their particular contributions. If I want to be sure they get the instruction, I have to direct my comments to them. Finally, when it's an error many students are making, it never hurts to repeat, repeat, and repeat, so they become accustomed to spotting and then addressing the error.

In synchronous classrooms, too, repetition is important. In teleconference classes, students have limited input from you—only your voice. In Webinar environments, they have more points of input, but also more distractions. The e-mail chime is like a cellphone ringing in a lecture hall. When you repeat the material you are most committed to teaching, it has a better chance of hitting the mark.

Provide Timely Feedback

Feedback is a critical step in the instructional experience of adults. Your students cannot effectively complete the process without your feedback.

Feedback occurs individually as well as in the classroom. If particular classroom assignments are due on a Monday, for instance, be prepared to respond immediately on Monday, at the latest, if only to the first few turned in.

Until students become adept at discussion and engagement, you may feel as if you are giving the same feedback over and over (which is good—you're repeating!): "Great comments. I particularly like how you described ..."; "Interesting. Have you also experienced ...?" Slowly, though, as the students become more comfortable, they will start to give each other feedback. And then you know you have created a classroom environment that works.

Some Are More Equal than Others

Even when students take on more responsibility for responding to their classmates, the instructor remains, in the words of one of my students, "The Queen Bee." As much as she appreciates what her peers have to say, she told me, "We're all waiting to see what *you* think of our work."

You can back off a bit once the students feel in charge, but you can never fully retreat. Interaction with peers, while wonderful for the learning experience and for creating a community of learners, does not replace interaction with the instructor.

Model Your Expectations

"Do as I say *and* as I do" needs to be your motto. If you expect students to adhere to professional standards of Netiquette, then don't make offensive or inappropriate comments in your asynchronous classroom. If you expect students to complete assignments in a timely fashion, then meet your own deadlines for grading and feedback. If you expect students to participate with depth and intelligence in classroom discussions, show them how by modeling the kind of participation you expect from them.

Frequent and clear communication on your part will set the stage for good relationships with your students and within the classroom environment. In the first days and weeks of a course, it is particularly important for you to be "visible" in the distance-learning classroom, providing thoughtful and responsive feedback to your students.

Manage Conflict

Throw any group of adults together and eventually a conflict or two will bubble to the surface. In my experience, distance-learning students generally bend over backward to avoid offending anyone (which presents a different kind of classroom management challenge since it can lead to milquetoast interactions), but someone, somewhere, somehow will spark a conflict. When it happens, you have to manage it in much the same way you'd manage it in a traditional classroom.

In the policies for my classrooms, I make it clear from the start that I do not tolerate unprofessional behavior, disrespect of students or instructor, foul language, or personal attacks of any kind. The first infraction results in an immediate response, gently in the classroom and a bit more firmly in private. For instance, I might interrupt someone who is cussing in a teleconference by asking the student to find more appropriate vocabulary for our discussion. I follow up with a private message, either on the phone or via e-mail, thanking the student for changing the behavior and reiterating my policy. In the follow-up, I always emphasize the open and trustworthy environment we are trying to create in the classroom. Additional infractions result in a sterner warning and other kinds of consequences—reduction in credit, for example, in a credit course. If necessary, I will remove someone from a class. I'm glad to say I've never had to resort to that measure.

I also try to steer dialogue away from hot-button issues, such as politics, abortion, religion, and the like, at least until everyone has gotten settled and feels comfortable. These elements are most likely to arise in students' personal introductions, although they occasionally crop up unexpectedly in other places in our discussions. I'm not opposed to discussion of challenging issues, but they do not generally relate to the content of the courses I teach. When discussions of this nature arise, I ask students to take them to a private space because the classroom is for course work. (If your course is about politics or medical ethics, I wish you good luck!)

Every now and then, I end up with a class in which two or more students are just plain hateful to each other. What can you do? They are chronological adults, but sometimes they just can't control themselves. Often these explosive relationships erupt not in the classroom itself but in learning-team situations—a smaller group setting, where difficult personalities are more likely to clash. But the impact is felt in the classroom too when some students start giving each other the cold shoulder or even making occasional rude cracks about each other.

If I can move them to different teams, I'll consider it, but first I contact them privately or respond privately to the one who comes to me first with, "I just can't work with so-and-so." Unless behavior crosses a line of offensiveness, I ask them, then *tell* them, to work it out.

In some classes, on the other hand, I long for conflict. It seems that every contribution from every student is cheerily positive. No one wants to critique anyone else's work, and no one wants to have a dissenting opinion. I want to shout at them, "How about a little passion, people?"

Many students are downright afraid of conflict, even of the most minor variety. To liven things up and keep the classroom from going silent, I sometimes deliberately introduce conflict. Creating classroom exercises around debate and role-playing can be very effective for introducing positive conflict; when students can dive into a role, they lose some of their inhibitions about disagreement. The resulting discussion pushes them further into the ideas we are wrestling with. Forced to defend a position, students think harder about the foundations of their logic or their approach to a problem.

Be Resourceful

Sometimes things just don't go as planned. An activity falls flat; the students are at each other's throats; the platform has a meltdown.

What do you do? Pull out your resources.

For every class I teach, I keep additional activities in my back pocket for each of the content areas. Field trips are always a good choice; anything that gets students out of the classroom environment is helpful when the classroom isn't running well. For Web-based classes, field trips can involve sending the students to find Web sites that meet certain criteria (e.g., non-profit, certain budget size, specified focus of work) and then report their findings to the class. For any distance-learning class, sending students out to visit a location in their area or interview another expert keeps them engaged in a different way with their learning.

Guest speakers can be equally distracting. A desperate call to a colleague, requesting 45 minutes to an hour of time, almost always moves a "stuck" classroom to unstuck status.

All the tricks I picked up in traditional classrooms for rerouting disappointing experiences apply to distance classrooms as well. And when all else fails, just know that this too shall pass—even if the students don't.

Create Culture

When you put all of these practices and ideas together, you are creating a culture for your classroom—one that invites, prods, and urges students to interact with the material, you, and each other.

Of course, all instructors have to be true to their own character and style, but distance-learning classrooms benefit from an abundance of warmth and human appreciation. Ultimately, the students will participate and will perform beautifully if they feel the classroom is a welcoming place, that is, if they are eager to become part of the culture you have established. If "going to class" is a chore, they'll find plenty of other things in their busy lives to fill their time. If, on the other hand, going to class offers a place to relax and get down to exciting work, if they feel appreciated and honored for their contributions, they'll find a way to participate despite everything else on their daily calendars.

Best Practices for Asynchronous Classrooms

Beyond the principles of classroom management that apply to all distance-learning environments, there are some particular considerations for asynchronous versus synchronous classrooms. Asynchronous classrooms are hard to imagine until you've been in one. "But how does it *work*?" is the most common question I get from prospective students. But once you've taught in one, you quickly come to appreciate the wonderful features and benefits asynchronous systems offer.

Keep It Organized

It's usually relatively easy to keep an asynchronous classroom organized—once you know how to do it. (Ay, there's the rub!) Most asynchronous systems allow for threaded discussions, in which replies appear below and indented from the original comments. Threads make it easy to tell who is responding to whom; you can follow a complete dialogue among several people simply by reading down the thread.

But threading is not exactly intuitive if you've never done it before. Listserv systems, in which the contributions are delivered to the participants' e-mail in-boxes, are notorious for creating confusion. Newcomers inadvertently hit "reply" when they want to respond privately to the contributor, and they soon find that their catty remarks about the instructor have been broadcast to the entire class. Newsgroup and bulletin board systems cause similar headaches when students swear that they posted in the thread, but their contributions are mysteriously "orphaned" somewhere else in the space. Threads are also easier to follow if the participants change the subject line when the direction of the dialogue changes, but even seasoned users are apt to forget this detail.

Some days I want to tear out my hair with frustration as I try to get the postings where they are supposed to be. But then I remember that for most of my students, this is a new skill set, like learning to use a word processor for the first time. Then I'm grateful that they're attempting to participate at all.

Organizational problems are not limited to the discussion component of a platform. In a collaborative Web environment, you might have students posting documents, adding a blog comment, or publishing Web pages all out of kilter with your guidelines. It can make for an extremely confusing environment, and as a result, students become frustrated and their participation drops.

In the first week or so, when I find contributions and materials in the wrong places, I often follow them with a threaded reply or comment such as this:

> Interesting comments, Xavier. I think you're on the right track. However, I'm going to ask you to repost this message in the designated thread. Threads help us stay on top of who is involved in the discussion, and they ensure that no one's contributions get lost in the shuffle of a busy classroom. Highlight the thread header, then hit "reply all" to post in the thread; let me know if you have trouble. ... Thanks!

If I need to provide additional one-on-one coaching for a student who just isn't getting it, I can e-mail, IM, or phone the student to review the steps of proper participation and my guidelines for interacting within the classroom environment. It's critical to provide guidance in a way that acknowledges the value of the student's ideas while instructing the student in how to use a tool. I also explain the value of the behavior I'm trying to encourage to the student because capricious rules bring out the rebel in many of us. If I focus entirely on the error or ignore the importance of the underlying reasons for a policy, I run the risk of insulting, embarrassing, or alienating the student—not a good move for our pedagogical relationship!

Use the Features

Asynchronous classrooms offer wonderful features that make any instructor's life so much easier. Want to know who has been participating and who hasn't? Set your viewing options to sort by contributor and date. Can't remember who made that thoughtful comment a week ago? Do a keyword search. Want to review classroom contributions before submitting final grades? Review them as thoroughly as you want: Every last comma is archived for you.

The features of the asynchronous classroom free me from the worry of remembering exactly what happened in class. I find that I can provide students with more accurate and unbiased feedback because I am responding to what they said rather than what I remember they said. I also archive the entire class discussion on a CD following the end of the course; if, 6 months later, I want to go back to a previous course and apply something that worked there to a current class, I have the archive to help me do so.

The ability of an asynchronous classroom to accommodate many different dialogues and activities at the same time is a feature I now find hard to do without when I go into a synchronous or traditional classroom. The multiple options mean that there's something for everyone; if one topic is dull or irrelevant to a student, there are three others they can dive into instead. In a synchronous classroom, it's one thing at a time.

Summarize and Send

The biggest downsides to the asynchronous classroom are (1) that it can mean a lot of reading and responding on the part of the instructor and (2) that it's easy to miss the nuggets of great thinking amid the multitude of words. In a busy class of 10 or more students, it's not unusual to log in and find 85 new messages to read through. Even if you respond directly to only a handful of them, that's hours of sifting and thinking as well as crafting your replies.

Students experience the same kind of overload. As the instructor, you can help them deal with it by summarizing the key points raised and discussed in the classroom for each topic or week of the course. When you do so, invite them to add to the summary: They can offer their own insights, including points you neglected to include, and their reflections on how they will apply these key points to appropriate areas of their lives and work. By doing so, you accomplish several pedagogical goals. First, you filter the wealth of dialogue into digestible chunks. Second, you repeat the key ideas you want students to continue to work with. Third, you encourage the students to do some self-reflection and additional encoding of their new knowledge. Finally, you help them transition their new knowledge to the world beyond the classroom. How's that for hitting a few events of instruction with a single little assignment?

Keep an Eye on Everything

Instructors in asynchronous classrooms should have eyes in the back of their heads, virtually speaking. If you have meeting spaces within the classroom for learning teams, let them work on their own, but monitor discussion in those spaces for appropriate, professional behavior; if interpersonal conflicts are going to arise, that's the most likely place.

Best practices for asynchronous classes call for us to create "chat room" space, where students can discuss anything they like. I usually keep a low profile in the chat room so that students feel comfortable using it even to complain about me if necessary. But I monitor it for language and appropriate behavior as well.

Finally, trust your instincts. If you sense that something is wrong (and it isn't just your own first-time jitters talking), follow up on it. Ask questions, probe for authentic responses, and ferret out the problems that may not be appearing in the classroom but are nevertheless affecting it.

Best Practices for Synchronous Classrooms

Maybe it's my age or natural inclination to written language, but I find it much more difficult to manage a synchronous classroom than an asynchronous classroom. When I'm leading a conference call, instructing through a Web-based synchronous environment, or even just conducting an IM tutoring session with a handful of students, I have a much harder time keeping all the balls in the air at the right times. The word "multitasking" takes on new meaning when I'm leading a synchronous program; at times, I'm operating equipment, delivering a talk, trying to type a reply to an IM comment by a participant, and checking the time to see if I've run over yet. It's no wonder I have more difficulty rerouting trouble when it comes up—trouble will just have to get in line for my attention! Such are the challenges of different media.

But (sigh), I know from my own experience that technology is mostly about becoming comfortable, not about the shortcomings of the tool itself. I run synchronous classrooms when necessary, and I become more comfortable with them all the time. Adhering to the following practices helps a great deal.

Have an Agenda

The worst synchronous classroom experiences I've ever had were the ones when I said to myself, "Hey, I've presented this talk a hundred times. I can go into the classroom and practically do it in my sleep." No matter how often I've presented on a topic, I go into the synchronous classroom with a detailed agenda: so many minutes for introduction and "housekeeping," my opening attention grabber, my first key points, my first question solicitation, and on through the final sign-off. I mark up the agenda with notes on progress; for example, I need to be at Agenda Item 6 by 2:55 P.M.; if I'm running late, then skip the second example.

The agenda is my lifeline. When I am instructing students through teleconference, the agenda keeps me grounded in instruction rather than simply talking about what I know. It reminds me that I'm managing a classroom. When I am instructing via Web-enabled conferencing, the agenda keeps me on topic and on track. Otherwise, I become too distracted by the tasks of managing the interface.

I keep thinking I'll outgrow the agenda, just as I once outgrew the training wheels on my bike. Now I'm starting to think the agenda is more like a safety helmet—the thing that will keep my head in one piece if my bike should crash.

Break Up the Presentation

It's a challenge when instructing through a synchronous classroom to stay focused on the students rather than the content. There's plenty of material to cover (there's always more to cover than you really have time for), so we tend to talk and talk and talk, and the students can absorb maybe a third of it all. When synchronous classrooms take on this character, they mimic the worst elements of the traditional classroom while lacking the guilty pleasure of letting us see who's wearing cute shoes.

Break up your presentations, much as you would for an asynchronous classroom. If you wouldn't make students wade through five pages of single-spaced lecture (and you'd better not), then don't make them listen to you for 60 minutes straight.

Fifteen minutes is a good chunk of time to allot for each segment of your classroom session. When you create the lesson plan, break up your material into single-topic chunks that you can cover in these briefer periods of time. Between topics, offer opportunities for students to discuss their reactions, present brief case studies, and even engage in a game or two. ("Guess That Voice" is one of my favorites for a teleconference; it helps everyone feel like we're getting to know each other as more than disembodied voices.)

Yes, I know these activities are eating into your precious time for presenting content. But the truth is that you will have more success teaching content if you break up your time and allow students to stretch their mental legs. (It's also harder for students to be secretly playing Solitaire or checking their e-mail if they know you'll be asking them to do something in just a few minutes.)

Keep to One Topic or Purpose at a Time

Synchronous classroom sessions should last between 60 and 90 minutes. If they run longer than that, I will bet you my gradebook that the students are not nearly as present as they may seem to be. Between getting started, breaking up presentation with activity and discussion, and responding to interruptions or questions, you don't have much time to present material. When you include synchronous sessions in your course, plan them so that you can cover a single topic or purpose in a short period of time on each call or online interaction.

Keep Your Cool

One of the things I most appreciate about asynchronous classrooms is that I can think through my response before I send it. In a synchronous classroom, I lose the safety net of the delay. If someone pushes my buttons or violates the culture I've tried to create for learning and exchange, it's very difficult for me to respond effectively in a synchronous classroom. My immediate response is not always a well-advised or graceful one.

I've gotten better at keeping my cool, mostly by training myself to allow silence before responding to just about anything. And truthfully, such situations have been extremely rare. In the interests of preparedness, however, it's helpful to have an idea about how you might respond if something goes awry.

Summarize and Send

As in the asynchronous classroom, students in a synchronous classroom benefit from the instructor's efforts to summarize the key points from a session and ask for additional input and reflection. It is good practice to send a summary to all participants following the session, either via e-mail or posted to a Web site or even via snail mail. The summary and invitation to reflect helps to free students from too much focus on note taking during the session and helps them encode their knowledge and apply it beyond the classroom.

Beyond the Classroom: Accept Feedback

Educational programs are notorious for limited assessment of their outcomes. Part of the reason is that it is confoundedly difficult to measure whether someone has "learned" something or not. Indeed, sometimes it's even difficult to determine what it means to learn.

Ability to assess the success of a program is predicated on the assumption that you have an idea of what success looks like. What should a student be able to say, think, or do as a result of completing the program?

Depending on the topic and type of program, successful outcomes might include the following:

- Succeeding at particular tasks, such as writing a professional letter or operating a piece of equipment, with a specific degree of accuracy
- Applying new knowledge to achieve an increase in revenues, volunteers, students, donations, and the like
- Completing a novel or collection of poems and submitting the manuscript to at least three likely publishers

If these look like learning objectives, that's not a coincidence. One obvious place to look for desired outcomes is the specific and measurable learning objectives you crafted in Chapter 3. It may not always be possible to assess whether the students have achieved the learning objectives until they have a chance to apply their knowledge in the field. That's why testing for knowledge serves as a substitute for true outcome evaluation in many educational situations.

But assessment isn't solely about what the students learned; it's also about the way they encounter and handle the experience of learning. Sometimes students learn despite our best efforts; sometimes our best efforts fall on sterile ground. To evaluate the outcome of a distance-learning program, it's also important to gather information about student attitudes, opinions, and reactions to distance instruction, particularly in the classroom.

Assessment can be a scary thing, which is why so many of us fail to do it. What if the outcomes do not tell us that we are being effective instructors? As painful as it can be to receive disappointing assessment results, the overall outcome is worth it; how can we ever improve if we don't know where we are failing?

At the University of Phoenix Online, students are asked to complete a substantial end-of-course survey, which instructors can review without identifying details attached. As a result, we instructors get a sense of how many of our students consider us to be "informed and professional" about our areas of expertise and how many would or would not recommend our courses to others. In Creative Writing in English, which founding instructor William Males is using as a laboratory for experimenting with online platforms and processes of teaching creative writing, students complete a brief evaluation monthly as well as a more extensive assessment at the end of each term.

It can be a humbling experience to review those end-of-course surveys, and I always do so with an attitude of openness and acceptance. The student with whom I butted heads for 5 weeks about the consistent lateness of her assignments and the erratic placement of her punctuation may blast me in the end-of-course survey. At the same time, I've found that these anonymous tabulations of strengths and weaknesses, covering content, interaction, and my teaching skills, have helped me become motivated to learn more about how to teach and how to help these students who want and need my help.

The end-of-course surveys and other kinds of student assessments keep me focused on improving my own performance and understanding student needs in my classroom. For example, several items in the end-of-course survey ask for student input on how well I create a professional and friendly atmosphere in the classroom. When I first read that, it got me thinking: What *do* I do to create a professional and friendly atmosphere in the classroom? Similarly, the items regarding how much care and concern I showed for individuals' needs and progress made me more aware of this issue from the student's perspective: What was I doing every day in the classroom so that each student would feel cared for and attended to?

In my consulting work, I'm often explaining to clients that conducting research or an assessment is about creating awareness as well as gathering data. By naming the variables on which you will be assessed, you create greater awareness in yourself and your students of the importance of those variables. Asking your students to assess your performance in the classroom gives you all an opportunity to reflect on what goes into effective instruction and classroom management.

Easy Does It—And Enjoy!

Lead gently in your distance classrooms, even while you push your students forward. If you are enthusiastic and genuinely concerned for your students' learning experiences, you can enjoy the process and invite them to enjoy it as well. Keep a copy of Worksheet 5.1 handy throughout the course; it will remind you of ways to maximize the classroom experience for your students as well as for yourself.

In the first few classes, it may seem as if you are mollycoddling recalcitrant students. But over time, you'll find that the handholding, repetition, and confidence building actually result in students who are more in charge of their learning experiences. You are training them to use the tools they need to succeed in your classroom and beyond.

Worksheet 5.1 Checklist: Practices for the Well-Run Distance Classroom

Prior to course launch:

- ☐ Review and edit (if needed) any classroom documentation
- ☐ Prepare all documentation for delivery to students
    - ☐ Post to asynchronous classroom
    - ☐ E-mail copies if necessary
    - ☐ Snail-mail copies if necessary
- ☐ Post instructor bio or send instructor bio via e-mail
- ☐ Set and communicate schedule for office hours

First day of class or initial classroom encounters:

- ☐ Greet all students on arrival
- ☐ Request bios from all students
    - ☐ Ask them to post to asynchronous classroom **or** -
    - ☐ E-mail to instructor for routing
- ☐ Assist with classroom usage issues
    - ☐ Call-in problems
    - ☐ Webinar connection problems
    - ☐ Access to Web-based space
    - ☐ Use of asynchronous discussion—threading, editing replies, etc.
- ☐ Respond to bios with probing questions about goals
- ☐ Make notes to student files on goals and personal details

During class (asynchronous):

- ☐ Review all postings
- ☐ Respond to deepen thinking and elicit discoveries
- ☐ Send positive feedback for substantive comments
- ☐ Watch tone to create encouragement, warmth
- ☐ Identify any potential difficult issues or personalities
- ☐ Post easy-to-find "questions" thread
- ☐ Monitor participation
- ☐ Summarize and send summary, at least weekly

During class (synchronous):

- ☐ Plan for presentation in 15-minute intervals
- ☐ Break up presentation with Q&A opportunities and group activities
- ☐ Focus on students not content during presentation
- ☐ Identify any difficult issues or personalities
- ☐ Monitor participation
- ☐ Summarize and send summary following presentation

Following class:

- ☐ Complete detailed feedback in a timely manner
- ☐ Archive class contributions for later reference
- ☐ Make notes for changes or additions for next time
- ☐ Conduct evaluation and request feedback

Chapter 6

Individual Learners

Although I've taught professionally for less than a decade, I've experienced the full gamut of emotions with respect to my students and their learning experiences: excitement, fear, maternal-like protectiveness, boredom, collegial good humor, annoyance, and more. There are classes in which I adore each student like a beloved cousin; there are others in which I can barely control my irritation with every last question.

Over time and with a great deal of soul-searching, I've learned that students reflect my own strengths and weaknesses in ways that are by turns dismaying and encouraging. When they bug me as well as when they thrill me, they are constantly teaching me about the limits of my power—as well as the scope of my potential—to influence others. The one who is pushing my buttons is usually the one who reflects back to me something irritating about myself (usually ego). And the one who takes every instruction and raises it to the next level of insight is the one who validates, humbles, and inspires me. The relationships I have with individual students are what keep teaching interesting. I'm constantly learning new things about myself.

Adult learners, as discussed in Chapter 2, bring their histories and experiences into the classroom. They have a firm idea in their heads about who they are as students. They tend to see themselves as primarily flawed or primarily outstanding, depending on how they experienced formal education while growing up. (Ours is not a culture that emphasizes balance.) I'm sorry to say that the majority of the students I work with tend to focus on their flaws at the expense of their talents (I blame insensitive educational practices for this sad state of affairs). As a result, members of this majority are insecure, anxious, and defensive—not a state that primes them for intellectual adventuring.

Students enter my classes carrying far more than one piece of baggage. My first job, before I can help them learn anything, is to stow that baggage. Luckily, the process for doing so also helps me create a personal relationship with them. Through that relationship, I can respond more appropriately to the particular learning needs of each. I think that's what's known as a win-win situation.

It's All About Them

When we first looked at the idea of students as the center of the learning program in Chapter 2, I shared with you my mantra: It's not about you; it's about *them.* The same principle is at the heart of building relationships with individual students. Learner-centered instruction means that it doesn't matter how expert I am in my field; it doesn't even matter how much work I've put into preparing an effective course. What matters is that the individual learner achieves a successful outcome. The learner is the purpose. I am an instructor only when I am in relationship with a student.

Being in a relationship means that I need to expend as much energy, or even more, on listening as I do on presenting information. Within the context of distance learning, listening involves careful attention to explicit questions and comments as well as the implicit information students share every time they contribute.

In a traditional classroom, the personal relationships I develop with many students are gravy—a nice benefit of our shared experience. In distance learning, on the other hand, I find that these relationships—and the work I put into cultivating them—take on a much more central role.

Why the shift? Probably because of the wider range of roles I play with distance students—cheerleader and mentor as well as instructor. Remember the model for motivating students that was presented in Chapter 4: The first step is common ground—we are alike. Until I know how we are alike, it's difficult for me to inspire. Once I know how we are alike, relationship is inevitable.

Getting to Know You

In traditional classes, I usually start things off with a quick round of introductions. By the end of introductions, I'm lucky if I remember most of the names and a salient detail or two about interests and backgrounds.

Little else sticks in my overstimulated brain, especially since I'm already worrying about what I'm going to say next.

Distance-learning classes start the same way. I ask everyone to provide a brief introduction—name, geography, interest and background in the course topic, perhaps where they are in a longer program of study, and any other details they want to share. I post my own introduction to start things off. A current version of my introduction, which I use with some variations for all classes, is included in the sample documents in Appendix B.

Since all my distance-learning courses involve some online component, even if it's just an e-mail exchange, I always make sure introductions are shared through that medium. Even if we kick off the course with a teleconference and do quick introductions on the phone, I ask students to do it again online. The benefit, of course, is that we have a written record of all those details, down to the number of pets and the ages of the kids in many cases, which is much easier to work from than my faulty memory.

From these introductions, I get plenty of information, both explicit and implicit. I get personal details—who is expecting a baby, who breeds German Shepherds, who has finally returned to formal education after dreaming of it for years—that help me connect in a human way to the individual students. A short comment like "How are the dogs these days?" dropped in at the end of a message can help a nervous student remember that there's a living, caring human at the other end of the line.

I also get information that the students don't even realize they're providing. With a scan of my eye, I can tell who will benefit from additional coaching in grammar and sentence construction (particularly important to know in my composition and writing courses). I get an immediate sense of the student's mastery of English (also important when I'm working so frequently with ESL students). I can even tell from students' use of paragraphs and line breaks how accustomed each one is to electronic communication; those who are most comfortable with digital connections use text formatting that is easier on the eyes—they've unconsciously mastered the creation of scannable material. Students with online experience also write sentences that feel more confident and natural—they've found their "e-voice." (I don't have data to support this insight, but I have yet to peg as a newbie someone who has actually done extensive online work.)

Perhaps most importantly, these introductions show me how ready and prepared each student is to learn and to work in partnership with me to get what he or she needs out of the course. Who is receptive? Who is defensive? Who is distracted by a recent promotion or a tangled divorce? All of these impressions get filed away in my notes—a spreadsheet in which I record all of a student's grades and performance notes as well as tidbits of information that will be helpful when I communicate with the student.

Tip for Managing Introductions

As helpful as the introductions are, I usually try to keep them out of our main classroom, which I reserve for course-topic discussion. For instance, at the University of Phoenix Online, I ask students to post their introductions in the chat room—the "anything goes" student lounge. This practice encourages everyone to use the chat newsgroup for other kinds of networking and casual dialogue while keeping the main classroom organized.

If a separate space isn't available, I at least work to contain the introductions in a single thread or a single set of e-mails. If our "classroom" is based on simple e-mail exchange, I often ask students to send their introductions directly to me so that I can manage their distribution, control the flow of data, and make sure that everyone gets the information. ("Reply" and "reply all" remain confusing to so many e-mail users, particularly at the start of a course. Did the introduction go to everyone or just to the last person who sent one?)

Being Proactive and Reactive

When I spot potential challenges (and they are always present), it's my choice whether to be proactive or reactive in response.

Some challenges require a willingness to react to what unfolds rather than an attempt to accomplish an immediate fix. For instance, a student who seems defensive and upset by the newness of the environment may just need a few days of practice to become more comfortable. If you immediately respond to a message with an offer of assistance, you might in fact reinforce the idea that the distance-learning environment is scary and difficult to master and requires that students get special help with it. By sitting back and letting students build their own confidence through practice, you let them find their own coping and adapting abilities naturally.

Other kinds of challenges, however, demand that instructors respond proactively:

- **Antisocial behavior.** Inappropriate language and disrespect of any kind get an immediate response informing the student of the ground rules for Netiquette. Subsequent problems require even more forceful action. It's impossible to establish an environment of trust with a loose cannon in the classroom.
- **Severe difficulties with written English.** Students whose initial contributions indicate serious trouble with written English require at minimum a "fact-finding mission." I usually contact the student privately to find out more. If I want to know whether English is a student's second language but the student does not volunteer the information, I might make my contact by telephone to listen for an accent. In most cases, once I've learned more about the student, my initial suggestion is simply some additional grammar exercises or tutorials. Other times, I probe tactfully for underlying learning difficulties I need to be aware of. This is a sensitive area, but if I can help a student tell me the nature of a special need, I can assist and accommodate the student within the parameters of the course.
- **Inadequate preparation.** If a student enters a course with dramatically inadequate preparation, it creates challenges not just for that student but for the functioning of the entire classroom. If it seems a student might have a hard time with the complexity or pace of the work, I try to work with the student to create a remedial plan. Very occasionally, I end up with a student who just isn't ready for the work. While I'm rarely able (for a variety of

contractual or political reasons) to ask a student to drop a class, I make a point of providing the student with particularly detailed and objective feedback, comparing his or her performance to the criteria for success. For everyone involved, it's best when an unprepared student drops the class.

But truly, the fun and pleasant discoveries about new students always outnumber the red flags. They all have interesting hobbies and histories; they tell funny stories and ask great questions. They may be wary of this newfangled distance-learning thing, but they are also curious, excited, and comforted by my warm welcome.

Enabling Customization

By the end of our first interaction, I know a distance-learning student far better than I know many of my traditional students at the end of an entire term. When I receive the first optional assignment—the completed learning-styles inventory—I know my distance-learning students even more intimately.

In Chapter 2, I discussed several online learning style inventory tools. When I receive reports from students with the results of their inventories, we can immediately turn what could be a content-centered program into a learner-centered program. When I receive the profile, I respond immediately with some tips on the best way for the individual to use the course materials, based on the techniques best suited to each learning style (see Table 6.1). I also let the students know which activities may be most effective for them, as well as which areas to watch out for. For instance, I always comment to solitary learners that the learning-team component of a course may be challenging for them. I take the time to explain the pedagogical reasons for learning teams, along with some of the specific skills they will develop by participating.

Table 6.1 Learning Style Advice: What I Communicate to Students

Style	What you will probably enjoy	What may be challenging for you	Strategies to try
Verbal	Reading lectures Reading class discussion (asynchronous)	Teleconferences and other synchronous events that cut down on text-based information Any graphic orientation to materials	Conduct a verbal analysis of anything that is challenging; use a keyword glossary; pair with a visually oriented student
Visual	Graphic presentations of information Whiteboard sessions (team or class) Mind maps	Reading text-only lectures and classroom discussion (asynchronous) Teleconferences with little or no visual information	Create your own mind maps of information; draw links among ideas, activities, and desired outcomes; "visualize" success
Aural	Listening to streaming audio Teleconference and Webinar sessions that deliver information orally	Reading lectures, content, and class discussions	Record key information and play it back for yourself; discuss concepts with a classmate or colleague
Kinesthetic	Doing activities that relate to the desired outcomes	Teleconferences and text-based content presentation (written lectures)	Pair with a verbally oriented student; suggest alternative projects and pathways through the course that speak to your learning style
Social	Participating in group work Participating in discussion	Independent projects	Form informal study groups if formal group work is not part of the course

Table 6.1 (*cont.*)

Solitary	Working on individual projects and reading assignments	Group work Participating in dialogue in the classroom	Role-playing; identify specific pieces of group work that particularly interest you and work at your own pace within the context of the group project
Logical	Analysis and pulling together ideas Whole-system simulations	Discussion that runs to superficial	Go as deeply as you are compelled to go with the material; probe in classroom discussion for more depth from classmates and yourself

Pairing Up

Learning-style information also helps you come up with fruitful pairings or team assignments for students. Persuading experiential or kinetic learners that they might get more out of the course by working in partnership with a text-oriented learner creates the conditions for success and satisfaction. In most of my distance-learning classes, I require my students to read and absorb a lot of textual information; I know that this emphasis will be frustrating to a kinetic learner. But a text-oriented learner will thrive, and together, the odd couple will succeed.

Motivation

By getting to know students as individuals—both who they are and what they are doing in your classroom—you gain an opportunity to motivate them in ways that have long-term effects on their success and, indeed, on their lives.

Many students move from class to class without a clear idea of what they are working toward. Without personal clarity and strong motivation, students get distracted, amass a body of credits and knowledge without knowing what it's truly for, and muddle aimlessly along. Focus and motivation work together. You can help enhance their motivation by working with them to

- **Clarify their goals.** Successful students identify specific reasons they want to be in a course or in a longer program of study and can describe what a successful outcome looks and feels like.
- **Internalize their goals.** Committed and self-aware students believe in their goals from the inside out. "My boss wants me to take this" is not an internalized goal. Neither is "A degree is just a piece of paper, but I can't get ahead without it." They need to be internally committed to the stated goals in order to stick with the course when things get tough. If the goal hasn't been internalized, over time they will become resentful of the pain and sacrifice of getting there.
- **Identify and achieve incremental successes.** Motivated students set and achieve interim goals that move them toward their dreams. Completing a single course, or even a single assignment within a course, is an incremental success. Motivated students also recognize partial success as success; completing a course with a less-than-ideal grade does not suck away all of their motivation.

For most of us, motivation is not a fixed state. We move along a continuum of motivation, some days feeling completely charged up and ready to take on the entire dream and other days feeling a bit more sluggish or unsure of ourselves. (I have worked with students and individuals for whom nothing seems to put a dent in their motivation; I want to know what they put in their coffee!) In getting to know your students, you'll get an idea of where their motivation is in general, but know that some days it may spike or plummet, possibly in remarkable sync with your cycle for returning graded assignments.

When I respond to student introductions, I often ask directly, "Tell us why you are taking this class. What are your goals?" I review their responses carefully for the balance between self-directed statements and external triggers. I also look for proactive motives (e.g., preparing for a new career or promotion) versus reactive motives (e.g., was told to build skills because of on-the-job deficiencies).

Finally, I pay close attention to the students who don't seem to have goals; they don't really know what they're doing in the course. The kinds of things goalless students talk about include the following:

- Vague plans of "getting a better job someday" (with no idea of what that job might be) and as a result being able to spend more time with their families
- A spouse, friend, or colleague who is taking classes and seems to be making progress

Or they don't answer the question at all. The students without goals are the ones I need to work with most to identify, clarify, and internalize motivators. They are the ones most at risk for dropping away from education without having an opportunity to figure out what they want in life.

Multiple Motivators

Even with a clear motivation in place, it never hurts to have another. With multiple motivations, students are able to reinforce their commitment to the work of the course.

Often, I see the need to build additional points of motivation when I'm working with University of Phoenix Online students. Since I work with them early in their course of study, they are fresh off the recruitment and enrollment process and still fired up that they're going to get the college degree they thought was out of reach. Yet the workload of my class is a surprise, and the degree is (usually) quite a long way in the future. I need to help them develop additional motivators that involve closer, more tangible

Table 6.2 Motivational Cues: Making It Work

Cues I get from student	Strategies to try to enhance motivation
Can't keep up with the work; too busy	Identify most important activities for each topic and prioritize with student on the basis of student's personal goals.
Lack of interest in topic(s)	Find ways to link topics with personal interests; customize assignments to allow student to adapt them to personal interests; link work to outcomes desired by the student.
Perceptible hostility	Call—personal voice-to-voice connection often helps; relax pressure on student to allow for acclimation; identify (if possible) root cause(s) of hostility and try to distance the cause(s) from the classroom environment.
Unprepared for complexity/focus of course	Suggest remedial resources, reading, and activities; pair with a "mentor" student, if possible.
Course isn't what student expected	Focus on desired outcomes—can student still get personal and professional value from course? Link activities to individual goals.
Reluctance to participate in group projects	Emphasize importance of distributed teams in modern workplace; highlight moments when insight comes into the classroom because of interaction; identify motivation (solitary learning style?) and suggest ways to accommodate teamwork.

goals to get them through the intense challenges immediately in front of them; the long-term dream of the college degree is too far away to keep most of them motivated through the pain and uncertainty of their first college research paper.

Strategies to Identify and Deepen Motivation

Since each student is unique, it's important to have a number of tricks up your sleeve to identify and deepen motivation (see Table 6.2). You never know what's going to be the most helpful until you are in relationship with a particular individual. The following learner profiles, which are based on composites of students whose motivation and learning quirks I have discussed with my colleagues ad infinitum, demonstrate multiple ways you can motivate students.

Learner Profile: Alissa

Alissa is a 35-year-old student at an international online university. She immigrated to the United States from the Dominican Republic nearly 10 years ago and is becoming more confident with her English skills while pursuing a degree in accounting. She also works full-time at a small accounting firm, where her innate math skills and can-do attitude have helped her advance. Alissa began her studies in part because her husband and boss talked her into it, but over time she has discovered that she really enjoys the process and is accomplishing a lot.

Alissa's motivation has shifted from largely external to internal. The instructor can build on this shift by helping her identify some specific directions she would like to take in her studies. She is enjoying college now, but naming and mapping out several short-term and long-term goals that are meaningful to her will help her over any bumps in the road. At the same time, Alissa needs to continue to improve her English skills. The instructor provides specific feedback relating to English structure and usage, as well as links to online resources for ESL support.

Alissa concludes the writing class with a C+ average, in part because she has more trouble with formal written English than with informal or spoken English. In final feedback to Alissa, the instructor reiterates the progress she has made and emphasizes that completion of the course is still a step toward her long-term goals.

Learner Profile: Mike

Mike is a 32-year-old student at an online university. He is returning to formal education after 13 years, picking up where he left off when he left his local community college to launch his full-time career as a computer technician. He is extremely successful and knowledgeable as a technician, but he has hit a ceiling for pay and advancement because he lacks a college degree.

Mike is skeptical that college has anything of value to offer him; he knows he is talented in his profession and feels that a degree is little more than a piece of paper certifying that he knows what he knows. In addition to a series of testy contributions to the classroom discussion, he responds angrily to the critiques in the first detailed feedback he receives from his instructor.

The instructor recognizes that Mike is neither truly motivated nor in a state of readiness to learn; he is defensive about any feedback he receives and does not trust the instructor or his classmates. To help him get past his defensiveness, the instructor calls Mike just to get to know him a little better. They chat for several minutes, not about the course, but about Mike's own career goals. A few days later, the instructor e-mails Mike an article from a business journal about the exploding opportunities in his field. The instructor is also careful, in all feedback to Mike, to draw clear connections between the class material and Mike's personal career goals.

Over time, Mike thaws slightly. He selects a research topic for one of the course assignments that enables him to discover new potential opportunities for his skills in fields he did not previously know about. He also develops a close relationship with a member of his learning team, who calls him to ask for advice about a recalcitrant computer system.

Learner Profile: Janet

Janet is a 52-year-old director of adult education at a large synagogue in the Midwest. She is learning marketing skills as well as investigating the possibilities of distance learning as a method for delivering education at her synagogue. She is excited about the opportunity to develop skills, but she is also buried in the administrative details of her organization. Furthermore, she has a difficult time feeling fully comfortable with the distance-learning format of the course.

After her initial introduction and greetings, Janet disappears from the classroom for nearly a week. The instructor e-mails, then calls her to find out whether anything is wrong. Janet is fine, but she's distracted by a new series of adult education classes that has just started at the synagogue; she's been trying to stay on top of enrollment changes for days. Plus her assistant is on vacation. The instructor reviews with Janet the two most important activities to complete by the end of the week.

Janet completes one of the activities and enjoys it thoroughly, but she doesn't have time to complete the second. She participates enthusiastically with her learning team and makes several new friends while they work together.

The instructor monitors Janet's progress closely. When she has time to do the work, Janet does exceptionally well; she is clearly mastering the concepts, and several of her activities turn into actual marketing campaigns for her synagogue's programs. But the instructor and Janet become discouraged by the difficulty Janet has balancing the course work and her job. By the end of the course, Janet has completed a little more than half of the assigned activities. She keeps the remainder of the activities in a "to do" file but wonders when she'll ever have time to get to them. In final feedback, the instructor notes that Janet has gained value from the course, even if she didn't complete all the work. She has gained practical knowledge and broadened her professional and social network.

Learner Profile: Daniel

Daniel is a 42-year-old active-duty soldier preparing to leave military life within the next 3 years. Throughout his military years, Daniel has worked as a medical technician; however, his lifelong dream has been to teach elementary school. He is pursuing an associate's degree through a military program that will enable him to translate military education and experience into civilian credits.

Although his long-term dream is clear, he is unsure of what he wants from the associate's program other than to get through it. It's taken him a long time to work through the required courses because the subject matter has not been terribly interesting to him.

The instructor contacts Daniel after reading his introduction and suggests that he organize all of his work for the course around learning more about elementary education. They talk through ways to adapt the assignments laid out in the syllabus to fulfill the requirements of the course while enabling Daniel to study and learn more about his dream job. Although some assignments, including learning team projects, cannot be adapted, the majority can.

Daniel becomes more engaged with the course now that he has a customized approach to the assignments. If there's an area in which he is less active, it's the learning team. He does participate with the team, but he puts his full effort into the individual assignments. Daniel's contributions to the classroom are refreshing to everyone because he has a unique perspective on the course content—he relates everything to preparing for a career as a teacher. The contrast between his responses and those of his classmates helps deepen the dialogue among the participants.

The Time It Takes

If it seems to take an immense amount of time and effort to focus on individuals and their needs, you are reading this chapter correctly.

Because effective distance learning is learner centered, an instructor can have a solid idea of how to instruct only by having a detailed understanding of the learners.

Over time, it becomes easier to identify what the trigger points for learners may be. You'll be able to review their introductions and their first few contributions to the classroom and have an immediate sense of a good approach for helping them. You'll also know just how far you can stretch your content and curriculum to meet learner needs without distorting your program beyond recognition.

Be Resourceful

No matter how comprehensive your courses are, your students will have questions and needs that go beyond its scope. While it's not your job to be all things to all people, you can be a hero by providing them with additional resources that meet their needs and move them toward their goals. As you learn about your students, be ready to pull out and offer resources that address what they need—you'll enhance their satisfaction with you and the course as well as push that motivation button!

For example, I maintain files with articles, Web links, and books that address the most common questions and knowledge gaps among my students. My files are heavily weighted with grammar and communication resources because I see so much need among my students for improvement in these areas. I have also created a guide for college students on Web-based research and information literacy; it includes links to reputable sources and a step-by-step introduction to effective use of the Web for research. At first I gave out that resource only on an as-needed basis, but I soon learned that "as-needed" really meant everyone. Now it's part of my standard toolkit.

For my marketing-for-nonprofits courses, I refer students to online discussions and listservs where they can pursue specific lines of thought or expand their work beyond the scope of my courses. Annotated bibliographies of journals, books, tools, and assessments are also in the file; rather than simply provide a laundry list of titles, I describe each item on the list so that students don't have to search everything to find what will be most helpful to them.

The team component of distance learning is challenging for many students, so providing them with additional resources on the how's and why's of team projects helps them work together effectively. Teams need to be able to create team standards, set agendas and deadlines, identify skills, and assign roles. Resources and instructions for doing so help them get off the ground. (Chapter 7 will provide additional information on the team toolkit.)

My own goal in working with individual students is to never have to say, "I'm sorry, but I can't help you with that." If I can always provide some sort of answer, even if it's just a referral to someone else who might be able to help, then I am putting the needs of the learner at the center of our relationship and digging into my resources to meet those needs.

Do You Know What You Know?

Organizing resources so that you can offer them when needed can be its own special headache. If you instruct in a single area of specialization, you might be able to organize your resources in a word-processing document or utilize your bookmarks or favorites to keep track of Web-based resources. Even within a highly focused area of expertise, however, the list can become unmanageable. For my own teaching work, which serves student needs in creative writing, marketing for nonprofits, Jewish organizational life, college composition and writing, English as a second language (ESL), and more, I need a better solution. Otherwise, I'd spend far too much time trying to figure out what I know and where to find it (clearly, my head is not the place for it all).

PowerMarks (offered by Kaylon Technologies: www.kaylon.com) and Net Snippets (www.netsnippets.com) are both good options for organizing Web-based resources. Both software systems allow you to capture information about Web-based resources and add comments, keywords, and other data. You can organize your resources in folders and search the contents by title, keyword, and more. It's also a fairly easy proposition to create a report from your data to e-mail to someone else—say, a desperate student.

Feedback

Individual feedback, both in the classroom and in private communication, can be the part of the learning experience that has the biggest immediate impact for students. In offering feedback, you respond in writing to specific assignments and contributions of the individual, place the individual's work in the context of the course overall, and compare the performance to the student's own goals and the established criteria for success. Feedback bridges all the elements of the learning experience and translates it into actionable information for the student: Where do I go from here? What's working? What could I be doing differently to enhance my own learning and performance?

Crafting substantive feedback is the most time-consuming part of instructing, which is another reason it is very important to have additional resources ready so you can point students toward other options. (Why go through the details of a grammar conundrum when you can refer them to an interactive Web resource?)

Every word is worth it, though. Feedback is one-to-one instruction, the meeting of the minds, the jelly next to the peanut butter.

Written feedback is preferable to oral feedback; even if you provide oral feedback during a formal conference, put your ideas, reactions, and suggestions in writing as well. Written feedback becomes a tangible document for students—something they can refer to over time to continue learning. Sometimes you provide guidance, for instance, on a skill or a task that the student isn't quite ready to fully absorb; if it's in writing, there's always the chance that it will emerge again when the student is ready to take that step.

Writing also forces instructors—myself included—to think through the instruction embedded within the feedback. Instead of simply telling a student, "This isn't working," we have to think through why it isn't working and come up with some suggestions for resolving the problem. I often tell my writing students that the process of writing doesn't just record thoughts; it also clarifies them. This is certainly true when I write feedback. I'm forced to support my ideas about the student's work. As a result, the student ends up with real information and personalized instruction on which to act.

The Feedback Sandwich

No one likes to be judged. Students experience a range of emotions—gratitude, anger, confusion—when they receive written feedback from instructors. Constructive critique and correction can be swallowed more easily when they are embedded in a "feedback sandwich"—a critique slipped in between two positive comments. For instance, I might comment on an essay turned in by a writing student:

> You've clearly given this topic a lot of thought, and you care deeply about the quality of on-the-job training at your office. It seems to me that a better organization of your ideas will help the reader follow the logic of your discussion—lead us from point A to point B and so on to the natural conclusion. (Revisiting and revising your outline will probably help, now that you've clarified what you want to say.) This is the kind of project you can definitely take to your supervisor when it's done and actually see change happen as the result of your analysis—let's get it ready for her!

Feedback includes specific positives as well as places for improvement. It even highlights an approach to improvement that builds on what the student has already done. The "sandwich" is completed with additional praise. As you develop more trust with your students, you can back off a bit on the sandwich approach, serving it "open-faced," with only an introductory positive comment before focusing on areas for improvement. But always lead with what the student has accomplished rather than what still remains to be done.

Sometimes building the sandwich is tough, especially when there is little to be positive about in the completed assignment or exercise. Still, it's worth the effort to serve sandwiches rather than humble pie if you want to keep your students motivated and involved with their own learning.

Which brings up another important point about feedback: The job of the instructor is not to "correct" the work but to provide guidance on how it can be improved as well as what is working.

Grading

If your program or course involves formal grading, your course materials must clearly communicate the criteria for grading. It's also a good idea to repeat the grading criteria for all major assignments when giving out the assignment. Standards should be consistent and, to the extent possible, objective. Create a process for yourself that will allow you to review student work, perhaps comparing an assignment to a checklist of excellence; apply the process for every student in the same way, for every assignment. Every now and then, I'll spot-check myself by regrading an assignment a day or two later, just to see if I give the assignment the same grade again (within a small margin of error).

Do not mistake grading as a substitute for substantive feedback. There's a huge difference between telling a student the work has earned a B+ and giving the student detailed information about what works in the assignment and what could have been done better. The grade should reflect the feedback, but the feedback is where the instruction happens.

Grades are important, of course, but I also try to emphasize that the process and learning experience are what truly matter. (I'm a fine one to talk, of course—I used to have fits over tenths of a point in my GPA .) One of the best students I ever worked with ended up with a C- at the end of his written communications class; he just didn't do much of the work in the first half of the class. Over the course of our work together, this student developed an entirely new approach to writing and revising his essays and discovered a latent gift. After I sent him his final feedback for the course, he wrote me to say that he knew he'd earned that C-, but he also knew he learned far more than the grade reflected. A year later, he was applying to journalism schools.

Grades can mean everything and nothing. When all else fails, they can be useful in stoking up motivation; more than once I've found that explaining exactly how a student could move from a C+ to a B put that student back on track in a course.

Keep It Private

Throughout the course, the relationship you build with each student is private. For the sake of trust, keep detailed feedback strictly between you and the individual. In the classroom environment, feedback should never get too personal.

For example, I never correct a student's grammar and punctuation errors in an asynchronous classroom. I focus instead on ideas, comparing and contrasting responses and providing additional guidance and insight on different lines of thought emerging in the discussion. I've found that correcting language errors is just too embarrassing for most students and causes them to clam up. In my private feedback to them, I discuss the most common errors in detail, encouraging them to use the resources available to practice new grammar and punctuation habits.

Privately, I can also push students harder. It's not unusual for students to start a class with great energy and enthusiasm, overflowing with dreams, but then kind of fade into the virtual woodwork when they can't immediately perform to their internal standard of excellence. The distance between current reality and dream just seems too great. In private feedback and communication, challenge them to work toward those dreams in spite of any disappointments or setbacks they may be experiencing. Return to their motivational points; remind them that each tiny step brings them closer to where they want to go.

It's Not Easy to Have Relationships

Despite the distance between us, I find that the relationships I have with individual students are highly personal, enriching, and satisfying. Unlike traditional classes, in which I might get to know a handful of students, distance learning requires me to make an effort to get to know them all.

It doesn't always work, of course. Sometimes it's downright impossible to learn much of anything about a student except an e-mail address and a habitual sentence pattern. No matter how you try to nurture it, no relationship blooms. In such cases, you just have to fall back on doing the best you can by teaching the content rather than the student. On the whole, though, I usually have a few authentic human-to-human interchanges with every student who shows up in my distance courses. Those interchanges form the core of our relationships.

Make no mistake though: Being in relationship with individual students does not mean you have to like everyone. In fact, one of the ways distance learning brings out the best in me as an instructor is that it enables me to work more effectively with people I don't like.

The "distance" in distance learning allows me to step back from the characteristics and personalities that I find off-putting and focus solely on the student's work. In a traditional classroom, it's easy to fall into the habit of avoiding eye contact with the student you dislike; in a distance classroom, you don't even have to pay attention to who is contributing a particular idea. When I'm leading teleconferences, I have a hard time distinguishing voices; in the online classroom, I may not even notice who posted a message until after I've read it. I've learned that a little willful ignorance allows me to respond to the work product rather than get sucked into unproductive personality clashes.

One of my first experiences with this kind of dynamic came in an online creative writing class. Not long after the terrorist attacks of 9/11, one of my students wrote a thoughtful essay comparing the United States to a codependent who is shocked when the substance abuser turns around and attacks. My first response when I read the essay online was entirely negative—I was offended, emotionally wrought, and ready to make that essay bleed red ink and beg for mercy. But I waited.

When I came back to the essay the following day, I realized two things: First, my initial response had been in part about my nervousness about critiquing this particular student, who often shook up the classroom with provocative statements. Second, I was not responding as an instructor to the essay. I owed it to the student and to myself to review the essay on its own merits, not on how I felt about the topic or position.

I still had plenty to quibble about in the essay—gaps in research, some questionable structure and transitions. But I provided feedback that evaluated how well the essay succeeded according to the aims of the writer. I made many substantive comments, and then concluded my feedback with a personal statement. I told the student about my first response, and how he had managed to spark strong, immediate emotion. To get past that emotion, however, and to create a writer-reader connection, I felt that he would have to make some substantial changes to the essay and possibly reconsider some of the prominent features of his argument.

For two nervous days, I heard nothing from him. Then I received a note thanking me for my thorough feedback and reading. While he believed we would not agree on his central argument, my response had helped him clarify exactly what he was trying to accomplish. I had instructed, despite my opposition to the statement he was making.

That was a powerful lesson for me in the value of critical thought over knee-jerk reaction and in what my role is when I guide students. I help them find their own voice, even if it's a voice I disagree with. A student information log (see Worksheet 6.1) helps me record observations that may be helpful in working with students as individuals and reminds me of the unique characteristics that each brings into our relationship.

As difficult as it sometimes can be to pull back from personality and focus on the work, it's harder still to get the students to do so. Yet it is critical for them to use teamwork in building their own community of learning and achieving a successful outcome. The next chapter looks at ways instructors can help that magic occur.

Worksheet 6.1 Student Information Log

I complete a worksheet like this one for each student in a class. I can use the worksheet to record participation and performance as well as any notes I want to be sure to remember when I write and send detailed feedback to the student.

Name:
E-mail:
Other contact:
Location:
(time zone:)
Bio information:

Stated goals:

Observations:
(language skills, attitude, needs, preconceptions, unique potential)

Sent learning styles inventory? Y/N
Learning style:

Team assignment:

Notes:

Chapter 7

Creating a Community of Learners

Private correspondence courses or mentored relationships rely solely on the educational value of interaction with the material and interaction with the instructor. A good distance-learning class, on the other hand, broadens and enriches everyone's experience by introducing a multiplicity of opinions and personalities into the mix through the third type of relationship in the distance-learning model: interaction with peers.

Building community is hard work. It may be the most difficult part of creating effective distance-learning programs. Learning communities face the same challenges as other kinds of communities: conflict, personality clashes, warring agendas, differing work ethics, cultural missteps, and more. Add to these the difficulty of working across time zones and with technology that puts many of us at a communication disadvantage, and it may sometimes seem easier to just forget the entire thing. Let the students interact with the material and the instructor, and leave the group stuff alone.

While this option may be tempting, it means ignoring a piece of the process that can make learning as engaging, relevant, and enriching as possible. For all its difficulty, the work you put into cultivating a community of learners will pay off for you and your students alike. To make it happen, you will need to provide clear, explicit, practical guidance to students on the right steps to take to become a community. (Yes, I know I've said that just about everything needs clear, explicit, and practical guidance—it's a running theme in all distance learning, where *nothing* can be taken for granted!)

Logistics and Psychology

"How are we supposed to do group work?"

I frequently hear this question during the first days of a distance course. Although this query is usually e-mailed to me, the whine comes through loud and clear.

To be honest, I'm pretty sympathetic to the whine; sometimes I whine too. The whiner doesn't really want to hear about instant messaging (IM) sessions, phone calls, e-mail discussions, or dedicated Web space for threaded discussions. The whiner knows these tools exist. What's really motivating the question—and the tone—is fear. The usual fears include:

- What if I get stuck with a lame team?
- What if I can't keep up with my team?
- How will we ever have time to do this team project when we need to use these awkward tools to communicate?
- I'm not even comfortable with this distance environment; who are these yahoos I have to work with? Do they know what they're doing?

My stomach knots up just reading these words. These are real fears that could strike any of us. The last thing Fear wants to hear is Logic.

In coaching students to work toward building a community of peers, my best resources are a willingness to let them air their concerns and my own experience with how, why, and to what end community works.

I let them complain. If I don't, they never get over it. But I also let them know I used to share these same fears and have come to appreciate what team projects bring to the learning experience. (Sounds a little like the motivational structure again, doesn't it? "We are alike.")

Psychology aside, the logistics do work. Working groups find ways to work at a distance for all sorts of projects. Conference calls, sessions, e-mail exchange, and file sharing, as well as dedicated online asynchronous discussion space (when available), are all viable options for teams to meet, share ideas, and make progress toward goals. However, unlike offline teams, distance-learning teams require a bit more foresight and planning, and you'll need to build enough time into the project calendar to account for the extra time that communication may take.

Creating Positive Peer Energy

The Creative Writing in English (CWE) course I co-teach through the University of Gävle in Sweden exemplifies the difference peer interaction can make in the learning experiences of both students and instructors. Now in its eighth year, the course has grown and deepened each semester as the students have forged incredible bonds with one another. The students find the interaction so compelling, in fact, that many remain with the workshop long after they have earned the maximum of four semesters' worth of credits the university allows them; they become official peer-mentors at that point, creating a middle ground between participant and instructor.

The CWE course truly benefits from the ongoing commitment of students *to the community of the course*. When new students first join, they can be timid about the many lengthy documents they have to review just to get up to speed on policies and procedures for participation. Seasoned students and peer mentors quickly welcome the newcomers though, and offer assistance and tips to keep them from getting overwhelmed. Throughout the term, many students meet face to face for group writing sessions, critique, and discussion. These offline connections add to the collegial, supportive culture online. In fact, students who are unable to participate in the offline meetings because they live in different places create their own local writers' groups to carry some of the online culture into their "real world."

The various elements of CWE have evolved over time and continue to evolve. Part of what makes experimentation and evolution possible is that the students deeply trust the community they've created, online and off.

Face to Face?

Is it easier to build community when we can see each other's faces? Probably. But that doesn't mean it's necessary—or even always a good idea—to add a face-to-face element to a distance-learning offering.

Blending distance and traditional approaches to education offers instructors a chance to combine the best of all worlds—a few physical meetings or class sessions for real-time, live discussion and instruction, combined with the features and flexibility of distance learning. When blending is done to enhance the overall experience of the learners, it can be a wonderful way to build community while retaining the benefits of distance learning.

Lacking the wherewithal to create an actual, live meeting, an instructor can turn to video conferencing or video-over-Internet solutions to create opportunities to "put a face with the name." Another solution is simply to ask all participants to provide a relatively small digital photo of themselves via e-mail or a post to a site.

But I want to make it clear that face-to-face elements—from the photo on up to the live meeting—are options, not baseline requirements, for achieving community. In many of my distance-learning programs, I don't even ask students to share a photo. Yet we successfully create a sense of shared purpose and culture that supports our educational work together.

Building on the Classroom Environment

Community begins right in the classroom. The classroom management techniques and tips covered in Chapter 5 begin the process of building a community of learners with the classroom as their "home base." If we think of a "community" as a location as well as an abstract collection of individuals, the distance-learning classroom serves the purpose of locating the group in the universe, just as a traditional classroom creates the logistical parameters in its own context.

When students enter the distance classroom, whether by visiting the online course platform, opening the e-mail discussion files, logging in to the Webinar, or dialing in to the conference-call number, they need to know what to expect and what is expected of them. They need to know what the community culture is, no less than what material you will be covering that day in class. The organization, protocols, and consistency you build into their classroom experience will go a long way toward helping them build community.

Still, even with the most organized classroom possible, the instructor has to put in overtime (particularly with a new group) to maximize the community-building potential of the classroom itself. Students are unsure of what to post, whether their questions really "belong" there, or whether they will be violating some unspoken rule that everyone knows about but them. Expect to be doing a lot of coaching and providing positive feedback for using the community space as a community resource.

A typical problem: I am facilitating an online discussion forum that is serving as the classroom for a program I developed for a client. I started a new thread recently for discussion, questions, and ideas relating to an activity that I'd previously asked all the participants to do at work. A few hours after I posted the message, I received a private e-mail from one of the participants: "I didn't know about this assignment; what are we supposed to be doing?"

I laughed. I cried. It was so typical of how nervous students ask privately rather than using the public, community space for questions. I posted a reminder to the public forum about where to find the assignment and what they were supposed to be doing. Then I e-mailed her privately, asking that she post a message in public asking for additional clarification. She did; I was thrilled. I thanked her in the forum, even as I responded to her question. A trickle of additional questions from other students followed. Everyone benefited.

I am quite sure that this individual was worried about asking something publicly that she supposed "everyone else" knew. But, of course, she was not the only one who had forgotten about the assignment or had questions on its execution. (Repeat, repeat, repeat!) At the same time, I don't want to be in the position of constantly "running" the classroom. Particularly when teaching adults, we have to create an environment in which they can take some ownership and control of the dialogue. Our goal is to help them become willing to post their questions and contributions without worrying that they will be judged negatively as a result—in other words, we want the students to see that their questions are actually the real purpose of the whole classroom enterprise.

Figure 7.1 illustrates how this very typical interaction plays out as a little one-act drama about community building. Community starts to put down roots when the instructor first creates guidelines and communicates expectations for participation. The instructor must also create opportunity within the classroom for community needs to be met—such as a designated place where students can put their questions and know they'll get answers quickly. Then the instructor has to step back and let the students choose to participate in the community. When private queries come in, the instructor can respond privately with encouragement but still direct the students to the designated community space. With specific coaching to help everyone contribute and public, positive feedback for success, the instructor can lay the groundwork for students to see the value of shared resources for themselves.

Group Work

Interaction within the classroom is an important step in building community, but it's only the first step. When all group interaction relates to classroom discussion or asking for clarification on individual assignments, you run the risk of having a more or less superficial discussion of the "I agree; let me tell you what happened to me along the same lines" variety. While valuable as a social experience, this kind of dialogue does not naturally enhance the learning experience.

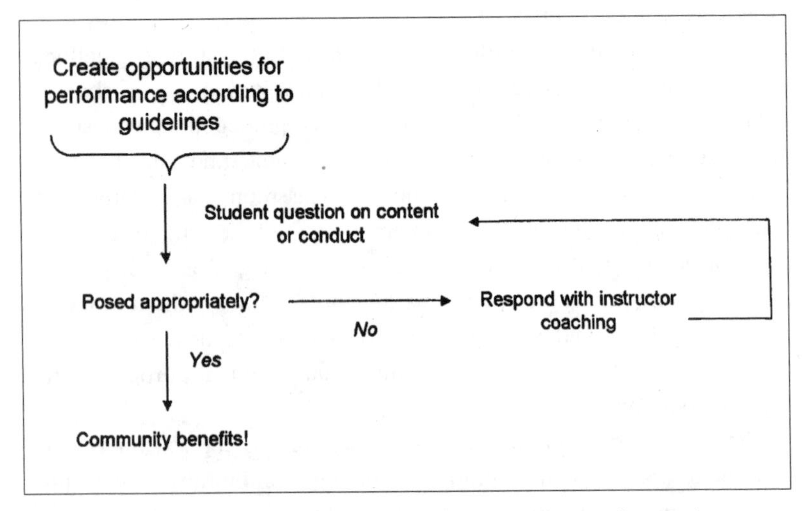

Figure 7.1 Nurturing progress toward community formation.

Another risk in the classroom comes when you are working with a large group, say more than 15 students at a time. Many instructors and organizations get excited about the idea of distance learning because they think it will allow them to reach enormous numbers of students with minimal resources and time. For community interaction to happen and for instruction to be effective, however, small groups are necessary.

My Creative Writing in English (CWE) course regularly registers between 40 and 50 students. We break them into working groups of about 14. Several students usually disappear after a month or two, so the working groups eventually average about 10 members each. Similarly, at the online campus of the University of Phoenix, undergraduate classes are designed to enroll up to 20 students. We break them into learning teams of four to six members to do projects together throughout the course, and the students come to rely on their teammates as a "community within the community."

Going beyond classroom interactions and getting students to work collaboratively on assignments has a profound impact on learning. When learners have to combine their ideas, skills, and experience and jointly create a product, they do more than master the material: They also learn about their biases and assumptions, strengths and weaknesses, and ability to help others succeed.

In a recent communications and writing class, I introduced a new team project I had never tried using before. The students were each given a worksheet with a long list of statements. I asked the students first to work independently to code each statement according to whether they thought it was a fact, an opinion, a value statement, or an assumption. Then, as a team, they were to compare their responses and discuss any they disagreed on. Finally, the team had to turn in a completed worksheet with their aggregated answers, along with a few paragraphs describing the results of their discussion.

The outcome was fascinating, for them as well as for me. The team discussion was particularly lively over the differences between opinions and value statements. In the end, they correctly identified all of the statements on the worksheet, but the most important element of the learning experience was the dialogue. All members of the team were forced to examine closely their assumptions about different types of information. Had they simply turned the worksheets in as individual assignments and received them back with my corrections, I doubt the assignment would have had nearly as much impact. Because they had to mull it over together with peers, they were able to teach themselves and each other in a lasting way.

Of course, team projects are sometimes disastrous. In almost every class, I get complaints from one team or another that so-and-so never contributes or isn't doing enough. Sometimes I referee personality clashes, feeling as though I'm separating 3-year-olds from the toy chest. Occasionally, I gently inform a student that he or she really does have something to learn from peers and that his or her skills aren't so far above the others as to make working with the team a waste of time. In one way or another, I have to work to convince students that the team component of the course isn't just a way for me to make their lives miserable.

Occasionally, team environments create serious problems. In one team situation, a participant plagiarized her section of an assignment, endangering the entire team's performance on the project. Although she owned up to the offense and accepted the consequences, her team responded by squeezing her out of subsequent discussions, making it impossible for her to gain any additional value from the team component of the class. On one hand, I couldn't blame them; on the other, I was stuck with a classroom management problem. I reminded the team that conflict resolution was a team responsibility, and they managed to get through the rest of the assignment together.

More frequently, clashes arise when one member of a team tries to take over the process or, worse, when two members of a team each try dragging it in a different direction. Private counseling with the warring factions is sometimes helpful, sometimes not. These are common enough situations, not just in a classroom, but also in a business, organization, or community. When I get complaints from team members caught in the middle, I remind everyone: The ability to work through conflict and collaboratively create a product, despite the challenges of distance and communication, is a life skill. Learn it now, or learn it later, but ultimately, it's not optional.

Get Them Talking: Stages of the Teaming Process

An ounce of prevention, I've heard it said, is worth a pounding over the head with a gradebook. If teams can get off to a good start, they have quickly built a teeny-weeny history of success. Any good experience is something to fall back on when individual personalities, fears, and egos start spicing things up. Just as I launch a classroom by creating a culture within it, I encourage and coach students to create a culture within their own teams.

The first stage of team formation is known in the organizational development field as "storming." This is the stage during which everyone is bubbling with ideas, offering their time, skills, and expertise to help the team reach its goals. Storming is also the "getting-to-know-you" phase, when team members start to share information about their preferred learning and working styles and see how they fit together as a group. Finally, storming can be a bit of a panic stage as well, when the team first takes a look at the project it has to tackle and is overwhelmed by the scope and challenge of it.

Following storming comes "norming," the stage in which teams start to get a sense of who they are as a working group. They begin to establish regular systems and protocols for working together. They become used to the idea of being a team, and they can break down a large task into component parts to build a workable plan. Norming is the stage when teams learn they can function without too much pain.

Finally, teams reach the "performing" stage, when they no longer think twice about how they will work together and simply do the work. It's similar to the final phase in learning a new dance step—it comes naturally and effortlessly, even if the dancer is perspiring like crazy when the music stops.

Teams move through these stages whether or not they have a process in place to help them do so. Unless they blow up for some reason in the storming or norming phase, teams will make it to performing. To help them get there more quickly and more effectively, a distance instructor needs to give team members a tool to create a community-based understanding of what they are trying to do, how they will do it, and the resources they have to accomplish their goals. This tool is known as the team charter.

A charter is essentially a descriptive document that lays out the team purpose, its members, the specific skills and resources each member brings to the project, a process for leadership selection and conflict resolution, guidelines and policies for meeting and progressing on the work, and criteria for success. Worksheet 7.1 shows a sample chapter, but any format works as long as the team members can use it to structure their work and interactions with each other.

Worksheet 7.1 Sample Team Charter

Course:

Team members:

Name	Phone	E-mail	Preferred contact and time zone

Team projects (review syllabus):

Project	Due date

Requirements for completing projects:
List skills needed, coordination of tasks, interim deadlines for reviewing work product, etc.:

Skills of team members:

Process for group work:
Describe plans for meetings, project leadership, criteria for individual assignments within projects, etc.:

Conflict management and resolution:
What potential conflicts may arise in the course of doing teamwork? How will the team identify and address conflicts?

Successful outcomes:
What will be deemed a successful outcome for our teamwork? (Focus on output rather than grades.)

All members of this team have reviewed the contents of this Team Charter. Our names added below signify our agreement to this Charter.

In most of my classes, creating the team charter is the first project I assign to teams. By creating a charter, teams accomplish a number of things that help them move through the storming and norming stages and get to performing:

- **Collective agreement on the nature of the task(s):** Team members tell each other what they think they are supposed to be doing. They create a shared understanding of the scope and nature of the project(s) at hand. If they find they disagree on what a project is supposed to be, they can contact the instructor for clarification (and I get a chance to see where my instructions still need a bit of editing).
- **Appreciation for and acknowledgment of unique skills:** In listing each team member's unique skills and resources, teams have an opportunity to see the richness of experience they have at their disposal. If they share learning-style information with each other as well, they have yet another lens through which to view the different ways they can approach a problem and solve it together. Reviewing the aggregated skill list can also be comforting to team members who are afraid that they'll get stuck doing an entire project on their own or that the project is too big to complete in the time frame allotted. A shared skill inventory helps teams begin to see themselves as a community that can take on more than any individual could handle.
- **Process creation:** Charters help teams divide large projects into discrete, manageable chunks and create a process by which they will complete them all. Even if the team does not follow its process exactly, having it helps members identify when they are moving off track. Psychologically speaking, having a plan takes some of the panic out of large projects.
- **Strategies for conflict resolution:** At the start of most team-building exercises, most teams feel that they will be the exception to the human rule that conflict is bound to happen. With the optimism of the start of a journey, they are sure that since they are all good people, they will naturally and with great maturity deal with any minor disagreements along the way. My advice is to always believe in the goodness of your teammates but also have

a plan for dealing with the inevitable. Putting conflict resolution into the charter forces teams to recognize that they will likely disagree somewhere along the way; they have a chance while they're all still on cordial terms to work out how they will resolve those issues. If they wait until it's a crisis, conflict can be crippling.

- **What does success look like?** Finally, the team charter helps members share and combine their ideas about what a successful outcome of their work together might be. There's nothing worse than getting three-quarters through a team project and realizing that you've been working on a presentation while your teammates have been working on a scale model. Shared understanding of the outcome not only clarifies what everyone is working on; it also helps teams budget their time and avoid wasted effort.

The charter process results in a document to which teams can refer along the way. It also gets them talking to each other and communicating on a very practical level about what they want out of their participation in the community of learners and what they bring to that community. At the same time, chartering emphasizes self-reflection. Individual members must think about specific actions they need to take to contribute to the success of the team. They cannot be passive on teams, and the charter helps them identify the unique contribution they can make.

No matter how well you support the formation of teams or working groups, you will experience resistance from some students. Many individuals have not previously considered their peers to be an integral part of their learning experience. They may prefer to be in the classroom, where authority is clearly held by the instructor, rather than in the team room, where authority must be shared. They may resent having their own performance depend on someone else's work. Chartering is not a panacea to the ills of teamwork, but it does help even the most skeptical feel like there is a route to success.

Peer Evaluation

Getting students to accept evaluation from their peers helps team members become more reflective and less reactive. When they know that they will be giving and receiving feedback using a formal peer-evaluation process, they take their teamwork more seriously. It's no longer something they're doing just to please the instructor or meet the requirements of the course; peer evaluation also serves to make them more invested in creating a functioning work group.

Peer evaluation also gives team members a way to begin talking about conflict while avoiding a personal attack. They can use an evaluation form to provide a team member with feedback that may be difficult to say directly. Asking a team member, "Why didn't you contribute to this phase of the project?" creates an adversarial relationship. On the other hand, providing a team member with an evaluation that states, "So-and-so did not contribute to the best of his abilities to the completion of the project," has more potential to open the door for dialogue about the situation.

I let students know, however, that I do not consider peer evaluations when I complete my own feedback and grading; I try to create my own impressions of a team dynamic without relying on the peer evaluations to keep me informed. Instead, when I review students' evaluations of their teammates, I turn the questions around:

- What could you have done differently to elicit optimum performance in your teammates?
- What did your teammates help you learn about yourself and your contributions to success?
- What worked well in this team environment?
- What will you try with your next team to achieve the results you want?

Thus, peer evaluation also becomes self-evaluation—an opportunity for students to understand themselves as a part of group solutions.

Making Magic

The mysteries of human relationships and community never fail to create intrigue. Chemistry can allow the oddest collection of individuals to come together and create something none of them expected. When personalities, learning styles, and tasks really mesh, it's absolutely magical.

The group comes together and has fun, learns the material, and turns out a great work product, and a few lifelong friendships develop.

An instructor can only do so much, of course, to elicit the magic. The final ingredients have to come from the participants themselves. But you can create the right environment for the transformation to happen.

One of my favorite tricks is to ask groups of students to do a small project together without informing them ahead of time that it's coming. For instance, if I have two learning teams responding to discussion questions, I'll ask each team to do a brief critique of the other team's response. The unexpected mini-assignment pulls them out of whatever dynamic they may have created in crafting their own response. It also throws them back into brainstorm-and-analysis mode, shifting them out of production mode. I've often found that these unexpected summonses (combined with an opportunity to do a bit of peer evaluation) bring out the best in work groups. They know how to perform together, and they discover they can have fun doing it.

Counterforces to Black Magic

If the magic in your community is of the darker variety, you have to do what you can to neutralize it. The plagiarist is one example of a bad situation, but there are countless others: the student who irritates everyone within e-mailing distance; the little dictator; the "whatever you want to do is fine with me but I'd better get a good grade" freeloader; the perfectionist who insists on doing every step of the project alone, even if it means redoing everyone else's work.

Distance communities require a high level of communications skill to be truly successful. And let's face it: There are plenty of poor communicators out there, and even those of us who make a living in communication can always use some improvement. Emotions can run very high within group-based projects. If you mix intense emotion with unskilled communication and pressure-cook the mixture in a situation in which everyone is struggling with new knowledge, the resulting dish can be pretty spicy.

Sometimes the best thing an instructor can do is let everyone back off for a few days. If the problem is within a small working group or learning team, I might even consider mixing up the teams; a new configuration of personalities may smooth things out. If explosions have taken place in the classroom, I devote classroom time (this is *my* environment too, remember) to discussing the problem as objectively as possible. I ask everyone to focus on what action we can take, not on what has happened.

Finally, I communicate, individually and to the dysfunctional team, that it isn't a question of whether they like each other. Rather, the objective is to achieve the community's goal: project output and successful completion of the course. It isn't much of a trick to achieve results when everyone is passing around the warm fuzzies. It's much harder to achieve results when we have to deal with opposing ideas, different ways of working, and competing approaches to the problem. If we can learn to listen and work around interpersonal conflict, then real change—in class, in community, and in the world—is possible.

Communication x Time x Outcomes = Community

If you have the luxury of working with a group over a period of time, or if you have a class made up of students who are moving through a program of study together, you have a wonderful opportunity to build a community that will exist beyond the parameters of your current course. Most courses I teach last between 3 and 8 weeks, which isn't much time for laying the foundations of community. Students gain terrific benefits from the group orientation of these courses, but they are unlikely to continue most of those relationships unless they are compelled to do so.

Time and continued progress are the differentiating factors between course-based community and long-term community. Distance-learning students who work together for 6 months or more get to know each other quite intimately. As they learn to function more efficiently, they can take on bigger projects and challenges, and doing so deepens their commitment to their community even more.

Instructors are also changed by the experience of belonging to this remarkable distance-learning community. Because distance learning puts us into relationship with so many types of people, it's a great arena in which to discover our own biases, soft spots, and assumptions about people. I have had many of my own subtle prejudices dismantled because I've participated in these communities. The personal growth and revelations that I gain from these interactions are what I've come to love about distance instruction. I can learn more about all the different ways there are to be a good person, to be a thinking human.

The most dramatic impact that participating in distance-learning communities has had on my own attitudes has come through my work with students who are on active duty with or recently retired from the military. Before working with these students, I didn't think much about the reasons young men and women chose military careers. In the past few years, I've worked closely with military students around the world and learned more about what it means to them to serve. I've had students keep up with coursework despite a last-minute deployment to Iraq; I've had students use my assignments to write for the first time ever what they saw, heard, thought, and felt while serving on missions in Haiti and Bosnia. Their perspectives, ideas, and words never fail to shake me up and remind me that mine is not the only way in the world.

Not every course results in the blossoming of community, just as not every student enters into relationship with the instructor. But by the end of most courses, the students are cheering each other on and working to help each other as well as themselves. They believe in each other, usually sooner and more easily than they believe in themselves. The strength they take from the confidence of their peers means just as much as the individual instruction they get from me.

Community building may never be easy. Students come into distance learning with an intuitive understanding that they will need to interact with content and with the instructor. Interaction with peers is less intuitive and needs to be proven through usage and results.

The amazing thing is that interaction with peers is the one element they can most easily take with them. Content and instructor are available only for the duration of the course. The more students come to see their peers as learning resources, the more they can continue to take charge of their learning beyond your classroom experience.

If you are lucky, they might even invite you to their reunions.

Chapter 8

Distance Learning as a Collaborative Enterprise

Learning occurs as a result of interaction. A learner encounters material, works with it, and in the process transforms it into new knowledge. Watch an infant or toddler for any period of time, and you will observe the process in action: Any interaction with the material world leads to experimentation, exploration, and natural learning.

Effective distance-learning programs are built on a foundation of carefully designed interactions. The most powerful distance-learning programs capitalize on three kinds of interaction: with content, with instructor, and with peers (see Figure 8.1). In this distance-learning model, students are not passive recipients of information; rather, they are the active center of their own learning experiences. To master new skills and knowledge, they must engage with the content of a course, interact with an instructor who can help them make personal meaning of the material, and validate and deepen their new knowledge through peer dialogue.

Before any of these interactions can occur, however, a different kind of interaction needs to happen: interaction among the collaborative partners who design, develop, and implement the program. Even the simplest and least technically dependent programs benefit from collaborative design and engineering. Because interaction is critical to the eventual success of a program, an interactive approach to development builds that orientation right into the foundation. You can't interact in a vacuum, nor can you create interaction from inside a vacuum.

The collaborative work that goes into planning, building, and implementing a successful distance-learning program has requirements similar to those of other kinds of collaborative projects. Individuals who are part of the collaboration must have

- Clear roles and responsibilities
- Shared understanding of goals

- Appreciation for how each contribution fits into the big picture
- Awareness of challenges
- Tools and processes with which to overcome challenges
- Ability to communicate
- Orientation toward problem solving

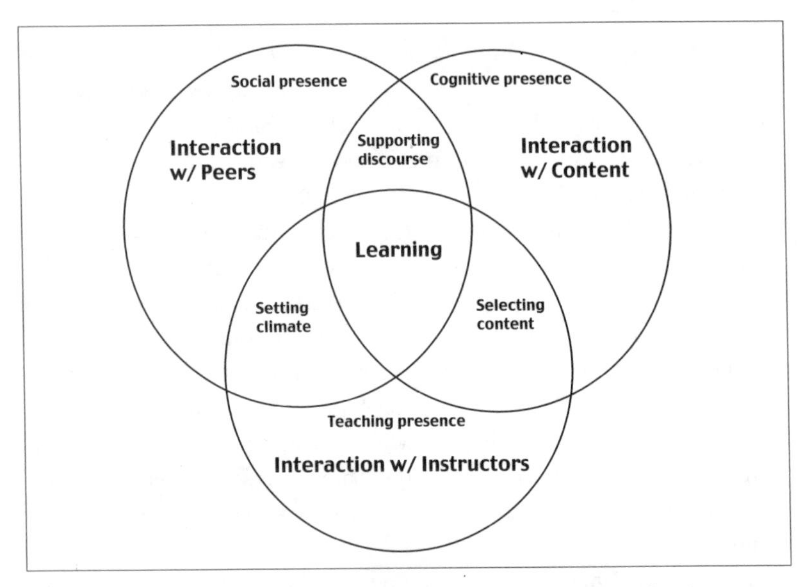

Figure 8.1 Interaction with content, instructor, and peers. The three kinds of interaction are what co-create an effective learning experience. *(Used with permission from Swan, Karen. (2003). "Learning Effectiveness: What the Research Tells Us," in* Elements of Quality Online Education: Practice and Direction. *Sloan-C: Needham, MA. Further information: www.sloan-c.org.)*

Roles and Responsibilities

Students and instructors are the primary actors in the distance-learning drama, but there are plenty of supporting parts to go around. Some roles and the tasks associated with them occur in sequence, while others can occur simultaneously. All these roles and tasks have elements that support both the instructor and the student, although some may have greater direct impact on one than the other.

How to Use This Chapter

This chapter is designed to be a stand-alone resource that instructors and their development partners can use to establish a shared understanding of their projects, roles, potential challenges, and desired outcomes. Worksheet 8.1 (on page 191) can help members of the team define their roles and understand the full scope of talent and resources involved in the project. Worksheet 8.2, at the end of the chapter, can be used as a discussion guide for team meetings or as a worksheet for each team member to complete before meeting. For further information and tools to support collaborative development of distance learning programs, visit the companion site for this book at www.electric-muse.com/tbyr.asp.

Figure 8.2 overlays the roles and work for the different members of the distance-learning partnership with the interactions that comprise the learning experience. Depending on the size of a project, the nature of the sponsoring institution, the budget, and the course platform, each role may be taken by one person, or some people may play multiple roles. For instance, in many cases the instructor is also the topic expert and sometimes the instructional designer as well. An administrative department or individual may serve as project manager and may also support the back-end needs of students and instructor alike.

The unique way each distance-learning project team comes together can create challenges if members of the team are not entirely clear on what their specific responsibilities should be. Teams run the risk of launching a project while missing critical skill sets if they do not start by establishing a clear understanding of who is at the table and what tasks each will be performing over the course of a project. To mitigate these risks, teams should complete a job description for each of their members. Comparing the aggregated job descriptions with the overall project plan provides an opportunity to identify any gaps or overlaps that could cause delays or communication glitches during the project.

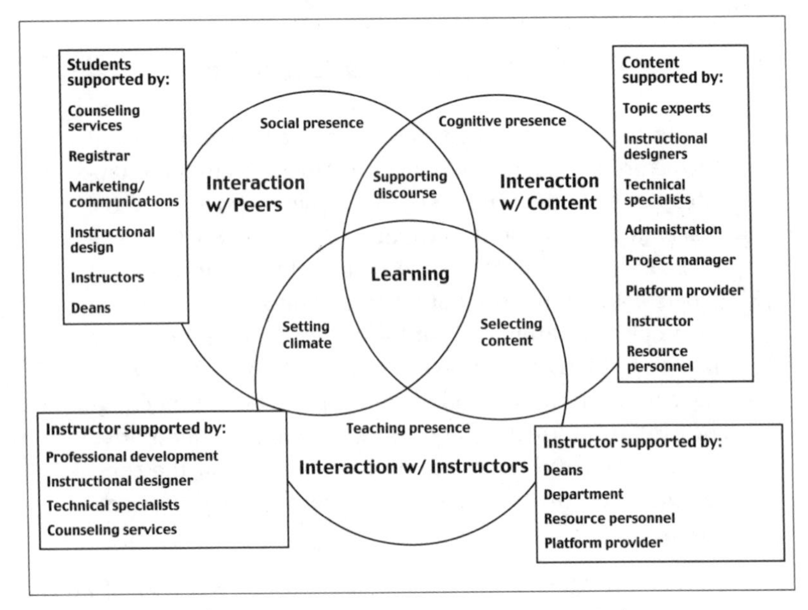

Figure 8.2 Roles and responsibilities to create interactions.

Content Roles

Before the launch of a course, a distance-learning team must first design, create, and test the content for the course. During and after delivery of a course, the team must assess the efficacy of the content, its usability, and its practical value to students and instructors.

The following team members are responsible for the content of a course:

- **Topic expert:** Individual(s) with expertise in the material students will be exposed to during the course.
- **Instructional designer:** Individual(s) with expertise in the design and crafting of instructional experiences based on learner needs.
- **Instructor:** Individual(s) who will present the content and help students interact with it to maximize their learning.

Worksheet 8.1 Team-Member Job Description

Name:

Title:

Essential role:

Skills required:

Timing:

Reports to:

Contact information:

- **Development expert:** Individual(s) responsible for packaging the content so that it is accessible to students and instructor during the course.
- **Administrator:** Individual(s) charged with overseeing content development and implementation tasks, maintaining overall quality and consistency standards, reporting on progress, and identifying process components that need to be improved, changed, or enhanced.

Administrative and Support Roles

Before the course is launched, team members in administrative and support roles document and market the course offering, handle registration, and arrange for access to the course. During the course, administrative and support individuals manage any technical support or access issues that arise, monitor attendance and grading if relevant, and gather and compile all formal feedback regarding the course. Following the course, the work of administrative and support personnel includes recording grades and credit, performing any course shutdown (including archiving) required, and distributing course feedback to other members of the team.

The following team members are responsible for administrative duties and support:

- Academic counselor
- Registrar
- Faculty or instructor development specialists or trainers
- Dean (or equivalent)
- Communications or marketing specialists
- Information technology specialists
- Student support services specialists
- Department chair (or equivalent)

Shared Understanding of Goals

With so many individuals participating in the collaborative work of building and launching a distance-learning course, it is critically important for everyone on the team to have a shared understanding of the overall goals for the project. Each project will have its own specific goals, but distance-learning programs must include the following among their primary goals:

- To create learning experiences that are **relevant, engaging, and challenging for students**
- To enable student **interaction with content, instructor, and peers**
- To foster student learning so that students can **achieve learning objectives**

It's easy, in the midst of the myriad tasks that occur during a distance-learning development project, to forget about the students and their learning experiences. Keeping these fundamental goals in mind makes the difference between courses that work and those that have terrific content and fabulous interfaces but fail to make a difference for students.

Beyond the fundamental goals, a distance-learning team must have a shared sense of the specific goals of its immediate project. Developing goals requires knowledge of the student population: What do they need to say, think, or do as a result of completing the course? What are the specific challenges the learner population may face in completing the course? What outcomes would be perceived as success by the sponsoring institution? The team may want to consider the following questions:

- **Research:** Is there a need, before developing the course, to conduct additional research about the needs and interests of the students?
- **Enrollment:** Does a successful outcome involve a specific level of enrollment? Would the course be considered successful if five students completed it? If 25 students completed it?
- **Capacity:** What scope of course complexity and student population are you equipped to handle?
- **Use of distance methods:** Are there particular methods and tools you are required to use to build and implement this course? Are there methods and tools you would like to try? What additional information do you need to make sound decisions about your methods and tools?

Establishing goals for the project at the beginning enables the team to evaluate its own success. Without knowing what you set out to accomplish, it's impossible to know if you achieved it.

The Big Picture

Once you have established a shared understanding of goals as well as the range of skills and perspectives represented on the team, you can assemble a holistic view of the distance-learning project and how each member of the team contributes to its success. Table 8.1 illustrates the interrelationships of tasks and events along the timeline of a development

Table 8.1 Tasks and Events on the Development Timeline

	Stage of process						
	Pre-concept	**Concept**	**Planning**	**Development**	**Testing**	**Course delivery**	**Evaluation**
Administrative roles		Establish budget, parameters, and resources for course		Market course		Provide support resources during course	Review course evaluation
Student support roles	Conduct enrollment; provide counseling	Gather input on need for course			Test with potential students	Interact with content, instructor and peers	Complete course evaluation
Content roles			Research resources and identify content experts; create instructional designs	Write/develop content and evaluations		Monitor during delivery and troubleshoot any emergency problems	Archive and document course

Table 8.1 (*cont.*)

Technical roles			Brainstorm tech needs; review requirements	Build and implement technical elements of course	Test and tweak		
Instructor support roles	Provide faculty development	Develop concept for course	Provide input on design and content	Provide input on content, evaluations, and technology	Complete training on course and platform	Interact with students; provide feedback; manage classroom; report any problems	Review course evaluation

project and how those tasks and events contribute to the goal of successful learner-centered instruction.

Where Are the Challenges?

Any collaborative project will face challenges—timing, budget, communication, technology, and contrary needs and perspectives. Members of the team have control over some of these challenges but not others. At some point, the budget cannot be budged; the technology can be manipulated only so far; project deadlines often have external triggers, such as the date that the new class of students is scheduled to show up and expect a functional classroom.

To be truly collaborative, distance-learning projects require that all members of the team approach the challenges with a problem-solving orientation. No one is allowed to get hung up on a problem! The creative brainpower of the entire team is ingenuity enough to get through just about any challenge as long as the members of the team perceive themselves as a team and not as competitors for limited resources, budget, or prestige.

When in conflict or just plain stuck on an intractable problem, return to the fundamental goals: relevant, engaging, and challenging learning experiences that meet the needs of students; everything else is secondary. With that priority established, reconsider the problem using the following questions:

- Does this problem interfere with the fundamental goals of the program? If not, is it really a problem?
- Is this problem under the control of a member of the team? If so, how can that team member resolve it? If not, how can the team as a whole neutralize its effects?
- Is there something missing that would mitigate or eliminate the problem?

Communicate

Team approaches to challenges can be successful only if team communication is successful. Clear and open lines of communication enable members to access each other's creative resources when needed. At the same time (and not incidentally), good communication keeps a project on target for deadlines and budget while helping a team *feel* like a team.

Enable communication by establishing protocol for use of e-mail, teleconference, shared online workspace, and other resources that draw members of the team closer together. Over the course of a long project, meetings for periodic updates keep everyone feeling connected and provide opportunities for group brainstorming about any challenges or issues that have arisen.

Be a Network

Distributed teams don't get the full benefit of teamwork if members do not have direct access to other members—if, for instance, all communication is routed through a project manager or other intermediary. For a team to "know what it knows," it needs to create direct-access opportunities among members. The project manager (or other central communicator) can be looped into the communications.

It's difficult, however, for members of a large team to have working knowledge of all the resources at their disposal. Network behavior is such that we tend to know our networks up to two steps from our own spot in the network: the "I know someone who knows someone" phenomenon. A point person, whose job is (put it in the job description) to know the depth and breadth of the team's skill set, can be the pivot that enables everyone else on the team to access each other. Figure 8.3 illustrates how this network model can help resolve a question or challenge that comes up in the development process.

Distance Learning Is in Beta-Testing

Despite impressive developments in the past several years and deep inroads on college campuses, in association offerings, and within corporate training and knowledge management efforts, distance learning is still in a cultural testing phase. Many distance-learning programs are designed and launched without much careful thought to what their educational role should be—or even whether the students are able to learn in this way. Organizations have a sense that distance learning can benefit them, but they haven't quite quantified (or even qualified) what that benefit could

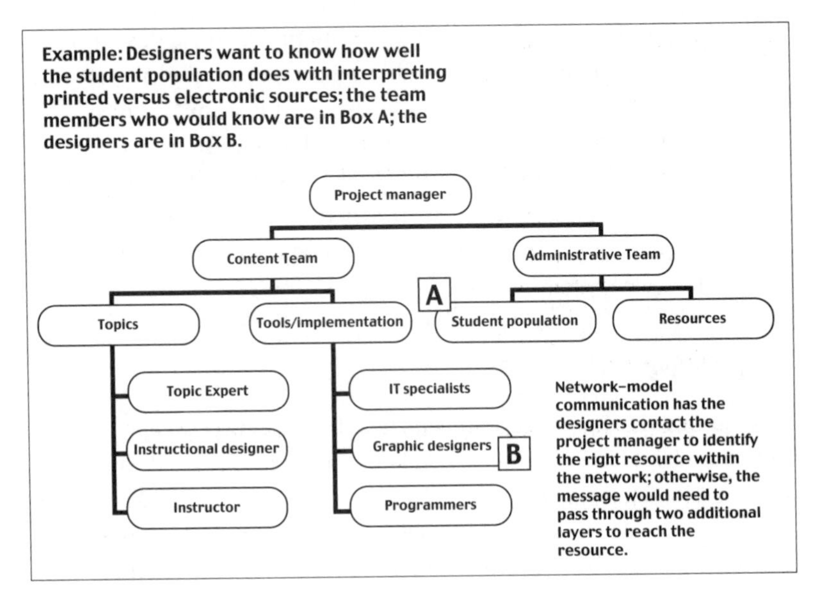

Figure 8.3 Example of a network model.

be. Cost savings are always high on their wish lists, as is the ability to serve a larger audience than with other forms of instruction.

On top of the other challenges inherent in any distance-learning program then, collaborative development teams face the overall challenge of focusing on a given project and tuning out the noise. A team can become distracted by the next hot thing—external or even internal pressure to go with a solution or move to a distance format because that's the direction in which the lemmings are rushing these days. Or a team can become distracted by the loudest skeptic in the room, who declares that it can't possibly work and that *this* educational problem can be solved only in a traditional learning environment.

The "distance" in distance learning describes geography; it does not require technology to be successful. It does, however, require a process-driven approach, a team of people who are willing and able to pool their collective wisdom and skill, sound instructional design, a method of packaging and delivering content, a student population motivated to learn, and instructors dedicated to connecting with students and establishing a classroom culture of learning. It requires a lot of support and creativity.

Interaction with content, instructor, and peers is essential. Everything else is extra credit.

What's your part in making it happen?

Worksheet 8.2 Worksheet and Discussion Guide: Distance Learning as a Collaborative Enterprise

Members of the collaborative team should respond privately to these questions, and then share their responses with the rest of the team.

1. Introductions

   Introduce yourself in terms of your role in the distance learning project.
   Example: My name is Robin, and I am the instructor for this course. My role is to co-create the content for the course and then facilitate the students' learning by helping them interact with the content, each other, and me.

   Does this description of yourself feel strange somehow? Natural?

2. Questions about roles

   What questions, if any, do you have about your role?

   Who might know the answer or be able to help you find it?

3. What are the biggest challenges for you in fulfilling your role?

   Challenges I have control over:

   Challenges I do not have control over:

4. Consider the challenges you have control over. What are two things you could do to neutralize them?

5. Consider the challenges you have no control over. What is missing that, if it were present, would enable you to overcome these challenges?

6. What are you most excited about in this project or course?

Appendix A

Resources and Further Reading www.electric-muse.com/tbyr.asp

A comprehensive resource list and bibliography would take more time to assemble than did writing this book in the first place. The resources, associations, and reading materials listed here are those I found most helpful in preparing this book and focusing my thinking about distance instruction.

Useful journals and Web sites published by an association are listed in the association's annotation. An updated list and additional resources can be found at www.electric-muse.com/tbyr.asp.

Advanced Distributed Learning, www.adlnet.org

Site owned and run by the Office of the Secretary of Defense. Deep library of useful articles, abstracts, and guidelines, including materials on compliance with the Americans with Disabilities Act requirements for access.

Allen Interactive, www.alleni.com

Organization founded by Michael Allen, author of the groundbreaking book *Michael Allen's Guide to E-Learning* (Wiley, 2002). Site includes registration for informative e-newsletter on e-learning, as well as links to additional resources.

Association for Educational Communications and Technologies, www.aect.org

International organization of professionals in educational communications and technologies. Offers online bookstore, free resources including Web-based journals, and e-books, conferences, and symposia.

Association for Training and Development (ASTD), www.astd.org

Conferences, networking, bookstore, and special-interest publications of interest to distance-learning instructors. Learning Circuits (www.learningcircuits.org) is ASTD's online source for e-learning research, marketplace, and resources. Includes excellent articles at many levels of expertise.

Australasian Society for Computers in Learning in Tertiary Education, www.ascilite.org.au

Publisher of *Australian Journal for Education Technology*, a peer-reviewed journal covering technology, instructional design, and education applications.

Capterra, www.capterra.com

Resources and references for tools and systems that enable distributed teams to communicate and collaborate. Includes capability for multiple requests for information (RFI) or requests for proposals.

Education World, www.educationworld.com

Resources in a wide range of areas relating to teaching, including technology, professional development, lesson planning, and others. Primary emphasis is K–12 but offers good resources for teachers of any age group.

Educause, www.educause.edu

Nonprofit organization dedicated to enhancing higher education through information technology. Conducts research, sponsors meetings, and provides deep resources in many areas of interest to distance instructors, including learning theory, instructional design, and technology applications.

Edutools, www.edutools.info

Clearinghouse of information, reviews, and best practices for tools and technologies to enhance education.

eLearning Guild, www.elearningguild.com

International organization of practitioners in e-learning. Includes numerous resources for developing and evaluating e-learning. Publishes *E-Learning Developers' Journal* and hosts conferences and online symposia.

e-LearningGuru.com, www.e-learningguru.com

Highly informative site owned and maintained by Kevin Kruse. Includes case studies, white papers, book summaries, and other resources. Sign up at the site to receive a free monthly e-newsletter.

FEASP-Net, www.sbg.ac.at/erz/feasp

Austria-based resource on making distance learning more emotionally sound. Includes research-based articles and information on emotional basis for learning and instruction.

Illinois Online Network, www.ion.illinois.edu

Collaborative project of Illinois colleges and universities servicing the global market in online learning. Offers online access to best practices, research, and articles of interest to instructors. Hosts institutes (online and off) for professional development.

Kolabora, www.kolabora.com

Online sources, reviews, forum, and expert referrals on online collaboration

LDPride.net, www.ldpride.net

Online tool about learning styles and multiple intelligences.

Learning Peaks, www.learningpeaks.com

E-learning guru Patti Shank's Web site, with in-depth resources and information on best practices, case studies, and resources for e-learning. Covers technical side of e-learning (how to design and build a site) as well as instructional components.

LTI Newsline, www.ltinewsline.com

Online journal with news, research, resources, and peer-to-peer connections in innovative learning.

Memletics' Learning Styles Online, www.learning-styles-online.com

Interactive resource to identify learning styles, including detailed information on the specific styles and how to work with them.

Sloan Consortium, www.sloan-c.org

Membership-based organization of institutions and individuals committed to quality online education. E-newsletter, research briefings, conference publications, and proceedings are all available via the Web site. Includes Web-based presentations on topics of critical interest to instructors.

Thinkofit.com, www.thinkofit.com

Reference and review of technologies for collaborative work space, forums, conferencing, and other tools with applicability to distance learning. Owned and maintained by David R. Wooley, a pioneer in collaborative conferencing and tools.

University of Wisconsin—Extension Service, www.uwex.edu/ces/pdande/learning/index.html

Division of program development offers many tools for instructional design and development for distance instruction. Of particular interest is the e-workbook Design for Learning—A Self-Paced Guide by Joan Cybela and Edrie Greer. Offers professional development workshops in locations throughout Wisconsin.

Appendix B

Sample Introductory Materials for Distance Learning

These sample materials are included to give you an idea of the way written documents set the tone for a classroom, clarify the expectations of a distance-learning environment, and guide students into the process of learning at a distance. I adapt these materials depending on the intensity, audience, and medium of a particular offering.

Additional samples can be found at www.electric-muse.com/tbyr.asp.

Item 1: Introduction

Upon completing registration for a course, a participant will receive a basic "introduction" message, usually via e-mail. Sometimes, however, the introductory message will be posted directly in a Web-based classroom in addition to or instead of the e-mail. The introduction message welcomes the participant and provides basic information for entering the class, accessing information, getting started, and identifying resources for questions and resolving difficulties.

Subject line: Welcome to class!

My name is Robin, and I am your instructor for this course. After you read this note, please hit "reply" to send me a short "Hi, I got it" type of message, just so that I know you're on board and ready to roll. You can also let me know at that time if you have any questions about starting up with class.

As you know, we will be using a Web-based classroom for this course. You can access the classroom by clicking on this link (or copying and pasting it to your browser if the URL does not appear as a live link):

[URL HERE]

Our classroom is a private, secure space. You will need the user name and password the school provided you in order to log in to the classroom. If you do not have a user name or password, if you misplaced it (don't worry—it happens to all of us), or if your log-in isn't working for any reason, please contact technical support right away and cc me on the message so that I know what's going on!

Once you are in the classroom, click the Syllabus link. This document will be your guide for the next five weeks. Read it carefully and completely. You might want to print it out if that helps you to absorb it better. You will be referring to your syllabus a lot during this course! All of your *assignments and due dates* are in the syllabus, along with other course policies.

You will find information relating to the first week's work by clicking on "Week One" on the Syllabus page or the Course home page.

Finally, visit our Discussion space. There, you will find my personal bio. After you read about me, please post a similar bio about yourself in the chat room by Tuesday so we can all get to know each other! I am looking forward to learning more about you! Some of the things you can include in your bio are where you live, what you do, some of your interests and hobbies, some of your goals, etc.

That should do it for now ... Welcome to class!

Item 2: My Biography

It is critically important that students feel like there is a real person at the other end of the line. I start every distance program by sharing my bio and asking that students share theirs as well. These introductions, which combine formal and informal information, accomplish several things. First, they create a sense of emerging community. Second, they give me critical information about who the students are, why they are in the program, what their points of pain and motivation may be, and other factors.

Subject line: Instructor Bio

Welcome to class! I'm Robin Neidorf (please call me Robin), and I'm delighted to be facilitating our work together in the coming weeks.

A few words about me: I've been teaching communications for six years, online for the past four, and I enjoy it very much. I've learned as much from my students as they learn from me—perhaps more! The range of perspectives we bring into these online classrooms really makes for rich discussion and interaction.

I've enjoyed distance teaching so much that I've written a book on it: *Teach Beyond Your Reach* has just been published by Information Today, Inc., much to my pride and relief! (Writing a book is a lot of fun but also a ton of work.) In writing the book, I've drawn on research as well as my own experiences at the University of Phoenix Online, the University of Gävle in Sweden, and the custom distance-learning programs I've developed and run for my clients in the field of nonprofit management.

I run a small research and communications business, Electric Muse. It's just me, my assistant, and my cat when she feels like keeping me company. I started the business back in 1996, following a checkered career in journalism, publishing, market research, legal services, and a few others I can't even remember ...

I live in Minneapolis with my husband, Andrew, and our daughter, Talia. And the supervisor-cat ...

But enough about me; I want to meet you! Please post your bio here in the chat room so that we can all get to know you!

Item 3: Time Management for Successful Participation

Helping new students understand how to fit distance learning into their lives is an important part of setting appropriate expectations and ending up with successful students. Another of my standard introductory materials is a "how to participate" document, sent via e-mail or posted in the classroom.

Subject line: Sample Work Flow for a Typical Week

To help you manage and plan your time, I am providing this sample work flow for a typical workshop week. Weeks run from Sunday through Saturday, with new materials posted to the Course Materials Center every weekend. This sample work flow is merely a guideline to give you an idea of how you could plan your time:

Sunday:

Check Course Materials Center and review new content

Print lectures

Review assignments

E-mail teammates with questions or comments

Monday:

Respond to an assignment in the Discussion

Comment on classmate postings

Tuesday:

Comment on classmate postings

Work with teammates on team project

Wednesday:

Respond to another assignment in the Discussion

Comment on classmate postings

Work independently on portion of team project

Thursday:

Comment on classmate postings

Begin reviewing insights and ideas of the week and making notes for Weekly Journal entry

Friday:

Final response to classmates

Finalize and post Journal entry

Update teammates about progress on project

Saturday:

Go enjoy some family time!

As you can see, it is very possible to be an active, engaged part of the classroom in small chunks of time throughout the week. Whether you have ten minutes first thing in the morning, a bit of time over lunch, or half an hour after everyone else has gone to bed, you can maximize your learning opportunities by logging in and engaging with classmates and the material.

Item 4: My Standard Introduction to Netiquette

Another posting that sets forth the tone that I want maintained in the classroom is my standard "Netiquette" message. It's a gentle reminder to pay attention to the nuances of written language, as well as a primer on some of the unique details of communicating in an online environment.

Subject line: A Few Words on Netiquette ...

Whether this is your first online class or your 100th, we all can benefit from reviewing appropriate "Netiquette," or manners for online communication.

The asynchronous online classroom environment offers us wonderful benefits—flexibility and depth, among others. However, we relinquish the immediacy of face-to-face communication, and the e-mail interface encourages "off-the-cuff" responses we may later regret.

When composing your messages, please be mindful of how your words may be received. Here are a few tips that can help:

- **Stay on topic.** While discussion is encouraged in our classrooms, rambling and off-topic conversations are not conducive to a quality learning experience. If you want to pursue a tangent, take it to the chat room, please.
- **Use appropriate subject lines.** As a conversation evolves, the subject may change, and it is helpful if the subject line is changed to reflect the topic addressed in the message.
- **Be attentive to editing your replies.** If you're responding to a message, quote the relevant and specific passage or summarize it for those who may have missed it. Do not make people guess what you are talking about, especially if you are responding to a particular message.
- **Maintain professional and respectful dialogue at all times.** Just as you shouldn't drive when you are angry, you should not send e-mail responses when you are mad at someone. Go ahead and type a response, but do not send it—just place it in your draft folder and look at it again the next day. Chances are that when you come back later to read your response, you'll be glad that you did not send it.
- **Uphold the standards of academic honesty.** Never copy someone else's writing without permission or citation, and always acknowledge your sources. We care about your ideas and *your* experiences. So tell us: What do you think? What is your analysis? What examples can you offer from personal and professional experiences?
- **Avoid "I agree" and "Me too!" messages.** It is very frustrating to find lots of messages with very little substance. Remember that e-mail communication can be "labor intensive" and that it takes time to read numerous messages.
- **Avoid the use of all caps.** (IT'S LIKE SHOUTING!) You can do it occasionally for strong emphasis, but only for individual words.
- **Recognize that we are "talking" with one another, not "writing to" one another.** Even though all of our

communications are in writing, it doesn't mean all of our writings are "formal" writing assignments and are, therefore, subject to the rules of written communication. Messages in the main classroom are conversation and are quite often informal (and prone to occasional grammatical, spelling, and typographical errors). However, despite that informality, we should still make the effort to transmit messages that are readable and understandable.

- **Contribute your efforts to building a collaborative learning environment.** As one of our facilitators instructs his students, "Be positive in your approach to others and careful about your words. Since we cannot see each other, it is hard to tell if you are bashful, bored, sarcastic, or just kidding. I expect you to be kind to one another and excel. You are not in competition for grades. Do not confuse winning a competition with meeting a standard of excellence. They definitely are not the same thing here. Use discussions to develop your skills in collaboration and teamwork."

Becoming an effective communicator in the distance-learning environment is important to your academic and professional success. I am happy to provide one-on-one assistance if you are concerned about your online communications skills. Please contact me if you have questions or concerns or want additional coaching in improving your skills.

Appendix C

Sample Lecture

This lecture, used near the end of my introductory writing classes, demonstrates how to apply the motivational formula to motivate students as well as present instructional information.

Arguing with Gremlins: How Not to Be a Writer's Block-Head

Who lives in your head?

A grouchy editor lives in my head. She's constantly nagging me to write more, write differently, write something else. She's quite convinced that every draft is worse than the one before, and she can come up with highly creative expletives to tell me what she thinks of the next one.

Step 1 of motivation: We are alike.

I listen to what this editor tells me every day. But I've also learned to tell her to shut up.

Most writers have someone like this living in their heads. (Some writers have several "head-friends," but that's another lecture!) In fact, no matter what field we are in, most of us have a little voice (or a big one) inside, constantly chipping away at our confidence in our own capabilities.

A friend of mine refers to these voices as the "Gremlins." This friend, a life-balance coach who helps working moms find balance in their busy lives, has taught me that the best way I can cope with my Gremlin-editor is to acknowledge her.

"If you ignore it or try to shove it away, it just gets stronger," she's admonished me many a time. "Respect that voice. Then tell it to leave you alone."

So when I work with writers and creative people of all kinds (which pretty much is everyone, since being human is a creative art in and of itself), I always ask: Who is living in your head? What particular scab in your psyche can your Gremlin pick? Once we've flushed the Gremlin out of hiding, we can cope with its message.

And then, with the Gremlin temporarily silenced, we can *write.*

Step 2 of motivation: Change is possible.

Writing Anxiety

Write a research paper . . .

Clarify your thoughts in a memo . . .

Send a letter to . . .

Summarize in a report . . .

Do you have a recoil response when you hear these kinds of directives? Stomach tighten up? Heart flutter? Do you get the sudden urge to clean your house top to bottom—just to avoid the task of writing?

Step 3 of motivation: The tools of change are available.

Writing anxiety is a common enough ailment; most of us experience it to one degree or another throughout our writing lives. Even today, a clean desk generally means that I have a major writing project due, and that I've chosen tidiness over effective time management.

Fear is specific; anxiety is generalized. With fear, we can name what it is we are afraid of; with anxiety, we only know that something has us unsettled.

The problem with anxiety is that it is unfocused. We know something is wrong, but we don't know exactly what it is. The first step in overcoming the anxiety is to pinpoint the source of the feeling—the fuel that keeps the Gremlin running around inside your head.

Here are the most common sources of anxiety:

- My grammar/punctuation/spelling stinks.

- A previous teacher (or several, or even a parent) always told me I was a terrible writer.
- I don't know enough on any subject to be able to write about it.
- Who's going to care what I think?

Did reading one of these phrases make you squirm? Welcome to the club!

We all enter the writing process with a double armload of baggage about our abilities, shortcomings, and history as writers. Once we have identified the source(s) of the anxiety, we can effectively counter the Gremlin's haranguing with the message we would prefer to give ourselves about our abilities.

At the same time, we can acknowledge the kernel of truth in what the Gremlin tells us. Certainly, we can all improve our work as writers and researchers. Show yourself and your Gremlin progress in your weak areas, and use your gains to build confidence.

Grammar/Punctuation/Spelling

What the Gremlin says: *Your grammar is awful. You can't punctuate a sentence properly to save your life. Don't even bother trying to spell correctly! It's a lost cause!*

The kernel of truth: Well, is this something you could improve on?

The course of action: Practice, practice, practice! In all communication, make an effort to use good grammar habits, and always double-check your written work for errors.

What you tell the Gremlin: *I appreciate your feedback. Yes, this has been an area in which I've had trouble in the past. However, I'm making a lot of progress through review and practice. No one expects me to be perfect ... except you, Gremlin!*

A History of Others Who Denigrate Your Writing

What the Gremlin says: *Mr. Brown was right all along! He hated everything you wrote in his class, and he made sure everyone knew it. There were other teachers too who didn't say it in so many words, but you always knew they didn't think much of your writing. You've always done poorly with writing, and you'll never improve!*

The kernel of truth: You may indeed have had teachers who condemned your work as hopeless. You also may have imagined criticism where none really existed. It's important to know that you cannot take away the sting of criticisms offered unkindly. Still, what's past is past, and skills improve with effort.

The course of action: Experiment with processes for writing and revision until you find a process that works for you. You can then have confidence in the process to take you where you need to go with your work.

If you are dissatisfied with the quality of your first draft, write a second. If dissatisfied with the second, write a third ... or start over! Again, the use of process for writing and revision gives you an action plan, no matter how awkward the first few sentences may seem.

Above all, stop telling yourself that you are a bad writer, no matter what you heard in the past. If you repeat this message to yourself, you are just helping out that nasty Gremlin!

What you tell the Gremlin: *So you too remember Mr. Brown! He was a character, wasn't he? It's too bad he didn't take the time to help me find my own process and voice as a writer. I'm sure he'd be surprised to see how far I've come in developing my skills. How I wrote in the past isn't relevant today; I'm a better writer this year than I was last year, and my progress will continue.*

I Know Nothing!

What the Gremlin says: *You can't write about* **that***! You don't know anything about it! How can you possibly make sense or draw any sort of conclusions when you're just a big ignoramus???*

The kernel of truth: Who isn't ignorant on most topics in the universe? Recognizing your own lack of knowledge is the first step in gaining knowledge and then communicating it.

The course of action: Research! No matter what the topic, you can plan and execute research to acquire the knowledge you need. Ask questions, identify and study resources, and learn what you need to know to address a topic well in your writing.

What you tell the Gremlin: *You're right. I don't know anything about it ... yet! It's great that I have a process I use to research new topics and get to the point where I'm able to write about them. Even when I work on a topic I think I know, research always teaches me something new about it.*

No One Cares!

What the Gremlin says: *You're going to pour all this effort into a report that no one will even read! Who's going to want to read what* ***you*** *have to say?*

The kernel of truth: Despite our sweat and tears, writing isn't always appreciated—or even noticed.

The course of action: Create a relationship with your reader to make even the dullest topic relevant and engaging. Know your audience; if you don't know your audience, find one, or make one up!

At the same time, write as if *you* cared about the writing. You can't make your reader care if you don't. Find the piece within your work you can be passionate about, and communicate that passion. Reach out through your words, grab your reader by the collar, and *communicate*.

What you tell the Gremlin: *That's certainly a possibility. But the work of communication is important enough to me that I am compelled to try. I care about my topic; I care about my readers. I hope this combination helps them care about my work.*

Gremlins Never Die

No matter how skilled we become in our writing, the Gremlins are always with us. Like everything else in the writing process, coping with the Gremlins can be accomplished best through a strategic plan, implemented step by step.

Step 4 of motivation: The result will be satisfying.

Know what your Gremlin says to you; know how to respond. Eventually you will find that, although at times irritating, your Gremlin can also spur you on to your best work. At those times, you are writing to please your harshest critic—yourself.

Appendix D

Copyright Considerations

Copyright is a deeply misunderstood issue within education circles overall and in respect to distance learning in particular. Because so many distance-learning programs rely on the Web to deliver courses or provide resources, instructors may be wading into deep waters if they do not fully appreciate the copyright requirements of electronic resources. Print-based distance-learning programs may also run into copyright issues if they incorporate photocopies or reprints of materials.

This overview is not intended to be a comprehensive review of copyright considerations; it is intended to alert you to some of the potential pitfalls and suggest ways to avoid some kinds of infringement. For more information, consult with the legal counsel at your school or institution, contact an intellectual property attorney, or refer to some of the excellent resources provided by Nolo Press (www.nolopress.com) on copyright. The Copyright Clearance Center (CCC; www.copyright.com) can assist instructors in determining who owns the right to material, securing reprint rights, and paying appropriate fees for doing so; the CCC's Web site includes helpful information and articles on copyright for educational and business uses.

Fair Use

Many instructors mistakenly believe that as long as they are using material for educational purposes, their activity falls within the definition of "fair use." While your use may fall under fair use guidelines, you should be aware of some triggers that cause you to have an obligation to request and possibly pay for permission for reuse and redistribution:

- **Profit-making ventures:** "Education," under the terms of fair use guidelines, means nonprofit educational institutions and programs. If you (or your sponsoring organization) are not a nonprofit, fair use does not apply to your educational programs.

- **Infringement on right of owner:** Your use cannot prevent or otherwise infringe on the owner's right and ability to use the material. This has been interpreted to mean you cannot take market share from the owner by using the material in a "fair use" manner.
- **Convenience does not take precedence:** If you are copying material to avoid paying for purchase or to circumvent long delays in delivery, you are probably infringing on the owner's rights. If you are relying on books and materials that are not readily available, you can request (and pay for) permission to photocopy those elements you need immediately.

Web-Based Sources

The convenience of the Web makes it tempting to reach out and grab whatever materials will enhance the learner's experience in your classroom. But the Web is not a copyright-free zone, and a site owner can come after you if you neglect to get permission for use.

In general, it's a good idea to link to a site in your classroom rather than incorporate content from a site. When you create links, be sure they open up a new browser window; you might also want to incorporate an interim page that informs users they are leaving the classroom and visiting an external site.

Even with linking, however, the safest approach is to secure written permission for any classroom use of materials. Know too that infringement frequently occurs on the Web in the form of copyrighted materials used inappropriately by other Web site owners. Someone else's misuse of material does not create an open door for everyone else to walk through; research the original owner of ideas, writing, and creative product, and get that person or organization's written permission to use it.

Creating an Example of Academic Honesty

In educating ourselves about copyright considerations and visibly adhering to the guidelines for intellectual property rights, we set the right example for students, many of whom are unaware that pulling material from a Web site is not an acceptable form of research. You might even consider creating a "guide to intellectual property" to help students who are conducting Web-based research understand the appropriate uses of other people's ideas and creative products. Then model the approach to intellectual property that you expect your students to follow.

About the Author

Robin Neidorf provides a range of research and communications services, training, and resources through her company, Electric Muse. In her client work, she often evaluates technical functionality to determine how to use those functions to further business, organizational, or educational goals. In reviewing the various technologies available for distance learning, she helps instructors and organizations understand how to use different functions without getting hung up on particular software packages or technologies that continue to undergo evolution.

In addition to her consulting practice, Robin teaches communications and writing through the online campus of the University of Phoenix and has co-taught creative writing online through the University of Gävle in Sweden. Robin holds an MFA in creative nonfiction from the Bennington Writing Seminars. Most of all, Robin loves to teach and enjoys having the opportunity to help other teachers learn to use the tools at their disposal to reach new audiences in new ways.

Learn more about Robin at www.electric-muse.com/tbyr.asp.

Index

Boxes, figures, and tables are indicated by "b," "f," and "t."

A

B

C

F

G

H

I

J

K

L

M

N

T

More Great Books from Information Today, Inc.

The Accidental Webmaster

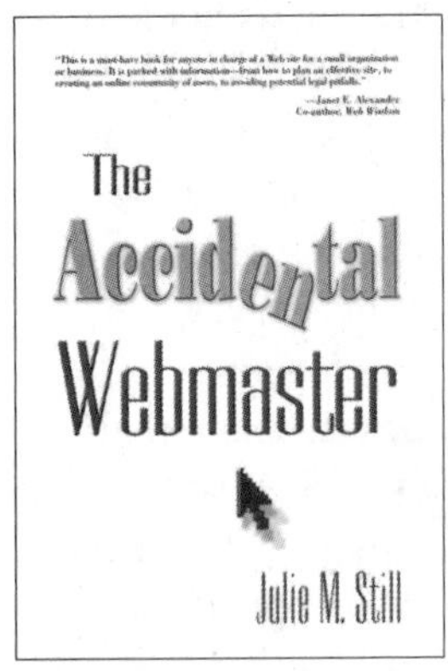

By Julie Still

Here is a lifeline for the individual who has not been trained as a Webmaster, but who—whether by choice or under duress—has become one nonetheless. While most Webmastering books focus on programming and related technical issues, *The Accidental Webmaster* helps readers deal with the full range of challenges they face on the job. Author, librarian, and accidental Webmaster Julie Still offers advice on getting started, setting policies, working with ISPs, designing home pages, selecting content, drawing site traffic, gaining user feedback, avoiding copyright problems, and more.

208 pp/softbound/ISBN 1-57387-164-8 $29.50

The Web Library

Building a World Class Personal Library with Free Web Resources

By Nicholas G. Tomaiuolo
Edited by Barbara Quint

With this remarkable, eye-opening book and its companion Web site, Nicholas G. (Nick) Tomaiuolo shows how anyone can create a comprehensive personal library using no-cost Web resources. This is an easy-to-use guide, with chapters corresponding to departments in a physical library. *The Web Library* provides a wealth of URLs and examples of free material you can start using right away, but, best of all, it offers techniques for finding and collecting new content as the Web evolves. Start building your personal Web library today!

440 pp/softbound/ISBN 0-910965-67-6 $29.95

Best Technology Practices in Higher Education

Edited by Les Lloyd

A handful of progressive teachers and administrators are integrating technology in new and creative ways at their colleges and universities, raising the bar for all schools. Editor Les Lloyd (*Teaching with Technology*) has sought out the most innovative and practical examples in a range of key application areas, bringing together more than 30 technology leaders to share their success stories. The book's 18 chpaters include firsthand accounts of school technology projects that have transformed classrooms, services, and administrative operations.

264 pp/hardbound/ISBN 1-57387-208-3 $39.50

The Wordwatcher's Guide to Good Grammar & Word Usage

Authoritative Answers to Today's Grammar and Usage Questions

By Morton S. Freeman
Foreword by Edwin Newman

Whether you write occasionally, frequently, in the course of your work, or just for pleasure, Morton Freeman's *The Wordwatcher's Guide to Good Grammar & Word Usage* is a book you'll want to keep within easy reach of your writing tablet or computer keyboard. *The Wordwatcher's Guide* is presented in a readable question-and-answer format, and arranged alphabetically by keyword for quick and easy reference.

304 pp/softbound/ISBN 0-9666748-0-4 $19.95